202 North Seventeenth Street
Allentown, Pennsylvania 18105

August 15, 1980

Feast of Our Lady's Assumption

Dearly Beloved in Christ:

      As Bishop of Allentown, it has long been my desire to have the children of our diocese, no matter what schools they attend, study and learn for life the fundamental truths of our faith as taught by the Catholic Church.

      To this end I now make the **BASIC CATECHISM** of the Daughters of Saint Paul an integral and mandatory part of the religion courses in every grade of our elementary and secondary schools, and in every phase of our Confraternity of Christian Doctrine programs. Further, I urge those instructing prospective converts to use this **BASIC CATECHISM** as their text, and I recommend that all families retain it in their homes as a ready reference.

      There is serious need, especially today, for all who profess the Catholic faith to know what the Church teaches. In their **BASIC CATECHISM** the Daughters of Saint Paul present this clearly and precisely, and I am happy to make it the religion textbook for all the children in the Diocese of Allentown.

      Asking God to bless you, I remain

Cordially yours,

+ Joseph McShea

Bishop of Allentown

BASIC CATECHISM

With Scripture Quotations

BASIC CATECHISM

With
Scripture Quotations

By the Daughters of St. Paul

St. Paul Editions

NIHIL OBSTAT:
Rev. Richard V. Lawlor

IMPRIMATUR:
+ Humberto Cardinal Medeiros
Archbishop of Boston

NOTE: Translation used is indicated each time by:

* New American Bible
** The Jerusalem Bible

Library of Congress Cataloging in Publication Data

Daughters of St. Paul.
    Basic catechism.

    SUMMARY: Presents the basic tenets of the Catholic Church in question and answer format with related scriptural quotations.
    1. Catholic Church—Catechisms and creeds—English.
[1. Catholic Church—Catechisms and creeds.
2. Questions and answers] I. Title.
BX1961.D27   1980   238'.2   80-149

ISBN 0-8198-0622-6 cloth
ISBN 0-8198-0623-4 paper

Printed in the U.S.A. by the Daughters of St. Paul
50 St. Paul's Ave., Boston, Ma. 02130

The Daughters of St. Paul are an international congregation of religious women serving the Church with the communications media.

CONTENTS

Everyone begotten of God conquers the
     world,
and the power that has conquered the
     world
is this faith of ours.
Who, then, is conqueror of the world?
The one who believes that Jesus is the
     Son of God.

1 John 5:4-5*

Prayers

THE SIGN OF THE CROSS

In the name of the Father, and of the Son, and of the Holy Spirit. Amen.

THE ANGELUS

The Angel of the Lord declared unto Mary.
And she conceived of the Holy Spirit.
Hail Mary, etc.
Behold the handmaid of the Lord.
May it be done unto me according to your word.
Hail Mary, etc.
And the Word was made flesh.
And dwelt among us.
Hail Mary, etc.
V. Pray for us, O holy Mother of God.
R. That we may be made worthy of the promises of Christ.

Let us pray. O Lord, it was through the message of an angel that we learned of the incarnation of your Son Christ. Pour your grace into our hearts, and by His passion and cross bring us to the glory of His resurrection. Through the same Christ, our Lord. Amen.

Glory be to the Father, etc.

REGINA COELI

QUEEN OF HEAVEN, REJOICE, ALLELUIA

Said during the Easter Season, instead of The Angelus.

Queen of heaven, rejoice, Alleluia.

For he whom you deserved to bear, Alleluia.
Has risen as he said, Alleluia.
Pray for us to God, Alleluia.

V. Rejoice and be glad, O Virgin Mary! Alleluia!
R. Because our Lord is truly risen, Alleluia.

Let us pray. O God, by the resurrection of your Son, our Lord Jesus Christ, you have made glad the whole world. Grant, we pray, that through the intercession of the Virgin Mary, His Mother, we may attain the joys of eternal life. Through Christ our Lord. Amen.

THE LORD'S PRAYER

Our Father, who art in heaven, hallowed be Thy name; Thy kingdom come; Thy will be done on earth as it is in heaven. Give us this day our daily bread; and forgive us our trespasses as we forgive those who trespass against us; and lead us not into temptation, but deliver us from evil. Amen.

THE HAIL MARY

Hail Mary, full of grace! the Lord is with thee; blessed art thou among women, and blessed is the fruit of thy womb, Jesus. Holy Mary, Mother of God, pray for us sinners, now and at the hour of our death. Amen.

GLORY BE TO THE FATHER

Glory be to the Father, and to the Son, and to the Holy Spirit. As it was in the beginning, is now, and ever shall be, world without end. Amen.

THE APOSTLES' CREED

I believe in God, the Father Almighty, Creator of heaven and earth; and in Jesus Christ, His only Son, our Lord; who was conceived by the Holy Spirit, born of the Virgin Mary, suffered under Pontius Pilate, was crucified, died and was buried. He descended into hell; the third day He arose again from the dead; He ascended into heaven, sits at the right hand of God, the Father Almighty; from thence He shall come to judge the living and the dead. I believe in the Holy Spirit, the holy Catholic Church, the communion of saints, the forgiveness of sins, the resurrection of the body, and life everlasting. Amen.

AN ACT OF FAITH

O my God, I firmly believe that You are one God in three Divine Persons, Father, Son, and Holy Spirit; I believe that Your Divine Son became man and died for our sins, and that He will come to judge the living and the dead. I believe these and all the truths which the holy Catholic Church teaches, because You have revealed them, who can neither deceive nor be deceived.

AN ACT OF HOPE

O my God, relying on Your infinite goodness and promises, I hope to obtain pardon of my sins, the help of Your grace, and life everlasting, through the merits of Jesus Christ, my Lord and Redeemer.

AN ACT OF LOVE

O my God, I love You above all things, with my whole heart and soul, because You are all good and worthy of all love. I love my neighbor as myself for the love of You. I forgive all who have injured me, and I ask pardon of all whom I have injured.

AN ACT OF CONTRITION

O my God, I am heartily sorry for having offended You, and I detest all my sins, because of Your just punishments, but most of all because they offend You, my God, who are all good and deserving of all my love. I firmly resolve, with the help of Your grace, to sin no more and to avoid the near occasions of sin.

HAIL HOLY QUEEN

Hail, holy Queen, Mother of mercy, our life, our sweetness, and our hope, to you do we cry, poor banished children of Eve; to you do we send up our sighs, mourning and weeping in this valley of tears. Turn then, most gracious advocate, your eyes of mercy toward us; and after this our exile, show unto us the blessed fruit of your womb, Jesus. O clement, O loving, O sweet Virgin Mary.

MORNING OFFERING

O Jesus, through the immaculate heart of Mary, I offer You my prayers, works, joys and sufferings of this day, for all the intentions of Your Sacred Heart, in union with the holy sacrifice of the Mass throughout the world, in reparation for my sins, for the intentions of all our associates, and in particular for the intention recommended this month by the Holy Father.

ANGEL OF GOD

Angel of God, my Guardian dear, to whom His love entrusts me here; ever this day be at my side, to light and guard, to rule and guide. Amen.

FOR THE SOULS IN PURGATORY

Eternal rest grant them, Lord. And let perpetual light shine on them. May they rest in peace. Amen.

GRACE BEFORE MEALS

Bless us, O Lord, and these Your gifts which we are about to receive from Your bounty, through Christ our Lord. Amen.

GRACE AFTER MEALS

We give You thanks for all Your benefits, O almighty God, who lives and reigns forever. Amen.

REMEMBER, O MOST GRACIOUS VIRGIN MARY

Remember, O most gracious Virgin Mary, that never was it known that anyone who fled to your protection, implored your assistance or sought your intercession was left unaided. Inspired with this confidence, we fly to you, O Virgin of virgins, our Mother; to you we come; before you we kneel, sinful and sorrowful. O Mother of the Word Incarnate, despise not our petitions, but in your clemency hear and answer them. Amen.

HOW TO SAY
THE ROSARY

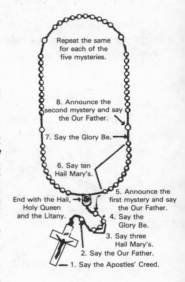

Repeat the same for each of the five mysteries.

8. Announce the second mystery and say the Our Father.

7. Say the Glory Be.

6. Say ten Hail Mary's.

5. Announce the first mystery and say the Our Father.

End with the Hail, Holy Queen and the Litany.

4. Say the Glory Be.

3. Say three Hail Mary's.

2. Say the Our Father.

1. Say the Apostles' Creed.

The complete rosary consists of fifteen decades, but it is divided into three distinct parts, each containing five decades. The first part is called the *Five Joyful Mysteries,* the second part the *Five Sorrowful Mysteries,* and the third part the *Five Glorious Mysteries.*

We begin the rosary by blessing ourselves with the crucifix and saying at the same time: ''Incline unto my aid, O God; O Lord, make haste to help me.''

Then we may say the ''Apostles' Creed,'' one ''Our Father,'' three ''Hail Mary's'' and one ''Glory be to the Father'' on the small chain. It is not necessary to say these prayers in order to gain the indulgences connected with the rosary.

The following is necessary: Meditate on the mystery, say one ''Our Father'' and ten ''Hail Mary's.'' This completes one decade, and all the other decades are said in the same manner with a different mystery meditated during each decade. Each decade is customarily concluded with a ''Glory be to the Father.'' At the end of the rosary the ''Hail, Holy Queen'' and the Litany of the Blessed Virgin may be recited.

THE MYSTERIES OF THE ROSARY

Joyful Mysteries

1. Annunciation of the Angel to Mary
2. Mary's Visit to Her Cousin Elizabeth
3. Birth of Jesus
4. Presentation of Jesus in the Temple
5. Jesus Is Found Again Among the Doctors in the Temple

Sorrowful Mysteries

1. Jesus Prays at Gethsemane
2. Jesus Is Scourged at the Pillar
3. Jesus Is Crowned with Thorns
4. Jesus Carries the Cross to Calvary
5. Jesus Dies for our Sins

Glorious Mysteries

1. Jesus Rises from the Dead
2. Jesus Ascends into Heaven
3. The Holy Spirit Descends on the Apostles
4. The Mother of Jesus Is Assumed into Heaven
5. Mary Is Crowned Queen of Heaven and Earth

Guidelines for Christian Living

THE TEN COMMANDMENTS OF GOD

1. I, the Lord, am your God. You shall not have other gods besides me.
2. You shall not take the name of the Lord, your God, in vain.
3. Remember to keep holy the Lord's day.
4. Honor your father and your mother.
5. You shall not kill.
6. You shall not commit adultery.
7. You shall not steal.
8. You shall not bear false witness against your neighbor.
9. You shall not covet your neighbor's wife.
10. You shall not covet anything that belongs to your neighbor.

THE TWO GREAT COMMANDMENTS

You shall love the Lord your God
  with all your heart,
  with all your soul,
  with all your mind
  and with all your strength.
You shall love your neighbor as yourself.

THE SEVEN SACRAMENTS

Baptism   Anointing of the Sick
Confirmation   Holy Orders
Holy Eucharist   Matrimony
Penance

SPECIAL DUTIES
OF CATHOLIC CHRISTIANS

1. To keep holy the day of the Lord's Resurrection: to worship God by participating in Mass every Sunday and holyday of obligation*; to avoid those activities that would hinder renewal of soul and body, e.g., needless work and business activities, unnecessary shopping, etc.

2. To lead a sacramental life: to receive Holy Communion frequently and the Sacrament of Penance regularly

— minimally, to receive the Sacrament of Penance at least once a year (annual confession is obligatory only if serious sin is involved).

— minimally, to receive Holy Communion at least once a year, between the First Sunday of Lent and Trinity Sunday.

3. To study Catholic teaching in preparation for the Sacrament of Confirmation, to be confirmed, and then to continue to study and advance the cause of Christ.

------

*In the United States, these days are: Christmas (Dec. 25), Solemnity of the Mother of God (Jan. 1), Ascension Thursday, the Assumption (Aug. 15), All Saints' Day (Nov. 1), the Immaculate Conception (Dec. 8).

4. To observe the marriage laws of the Church: to give religious training (by example and word) to one's children; to use parish schools and religious education programs.

5. To strengthen and support the Church: one's own parish community and parish priests; the world-wide Church and the Holy Father.

6. To do penance, including abstaining from meat and fasting from food on the appointed days.

7. To join in the missionary spirit and apostolate of the Church.

THE EIGHT BEATITUDES

1. Blest are the poor in spirit: the reign of God is theirs.
2. Blest too are the sorrowing; they shall be consoled.
3. [Blest are the lowly; they shall inherit the land.]
4. Blest are they who hunger and thirst for holiness; they shall have their fill.
5. Blest are they who show mercy; mercy shall be theirs.
6. Blest are the single-hearted for they shall see God.
7. Blest too the peacemakers; they shall be called sons of God.
8. Blest are those persecuted for holiness' sake; the reign of God is theirs.   Mt. 5:3-10*

THE WORKS OF MERCY

Spiritual

1. To admonish the sinner
2. To instruct the ignorant
3. To counsel the doubtful

4. To comfort the sorrowful
5. To bear wrongs patiently
6. To forgive all injuries
7. To pray for the living and the dead

Corporal

1. To feed the hungry
2. To give drink to the thirsty
3. To clothe the naked
4. To visit the imprisoned
5. To shelter the homeless
6. To visit the sick
7. To bury the dead

GIFTS OF THE HOLY SPIRIT

wisdom
understanding
counsel (right judgment)
fortitude (courage)
knowledge
piety (love)
fear of the Lord (reverence)

FRUITS OF THE HOLY SPIRIT

charity
joy
peace
patience
kindness
goodness

long-suffering
humility
fidelity
modesty
continence
chastity

What We Believe

HOW WE KNOW ABOUT GOD

IS THERE A GOD?

Yes, there is a God.

There is...one God who is Father of all, over all, through all and within all (Eph. 4:5-6).**

WHO IS GOD?

God is the all-powerful Spirit who created everything that makes up the universe. He is our Father who is with us always and awaits us in heaven to share His everlasting joys with us.

"[He is] the God who made the world and all that is in it..." (Acts 17:24).*

IS GOD REAL AND LIVING?

Yes, God is real and living.

HOW CAN WE KNOW THAT THERE IS A GOD?

We can know that there is a God through reason and revelation.

WHAT DO WE MEAN BY REASON?

By "reason" we mean our power to think.

WHAT ARE SOME OF THE WAYS GOD'S EXISTENCE CAN BE KNOWN BY OUR POWER TO THINK AND REASON?

We can know about God's existence from nature's laws and purposes, the degrees of perfection in the universe, motion, causes and effects, and changing beings. The Bible puts this question to us:

> For if they [men] so far succeeded in knowledge
>   that they could speculate about the world,
>   how did they not more quickly find its Lord? (Wis. 13:9)*

DO THE MAGNIFICENT UNIVERSE AND OUR WORLD POINT TO A CREATOR?

Yes, the magnificent universe and our world point to the Creator. St. Paul says:

> Ever since God created the world his everlasting power and deity—however invisible—have been there for the mind to see in the things he has made (Rom. 1:20).** (See also: Rom. 11:36.)

ARE THERE OTHER RELIGIOUS FACTS THAT WE CAN KNOW BY THE USE OF OUR REASON?

Yes, there are other religious facts that we can know by the use of our reason. These are some of them:

—the human soul will never die (see page 37).

—everyone has a duty to worship God, who created us (see pages 165-167).

—the Gospels are real, historical books, worthy of being believed (see page 43).

Therefore, it is reasonable to believe that God revealed Himself through Jesus and reasonable to join the Church that Jesus founded, as we shall see throughout this *Basic Catechism.*

WHAT IS GOD'S REVELATION?

God's revelation is what He has told us about Himself, ourselves and His plan of love for us. *Revelation* is the sum of the truths of religion which God has made known to us through Scripture and Tradition. (Scripture: see pages 41-43; Tradition: see pages 43-44.)

WHY DO WE NEED GOD'S REVELATION?

We need God's revelation because without His help our reason (thinking power) could not discover everything that God wants us to know about Himself, ourselves and His plan of love for us which is for our present life and the life to come.

HOW HAS GOD GIVEN US HIS REVELATION?

God has given us His revelation through His Son, Jesus Christ, who is God-made-man. He has also revealed Himself through the Bible, divine Tradition and the teachings of the Church.

WHAT IS MEANT BY THE "DEPOSIT OF FAITH"?

By the "Deposit of Faith" is meant the truths which God has revealed and has given to His Church to keep and to teach.

WHAT ARE OUR REASONS FOR BELIEVING WHAT GOD HAS REVEALED?

We believe what God has revealed because we are His creatures and He loves us. He knows all things, desires our good and would never lead us astray.

WHAT IS FAITH?

Faith is a gift from God by which we believe what He has revealed.

...Without faith, it is impossible to please him. Anyone who comes to God must believe that he exists, and that he rewards those who seek him (Heb. 11:6).*

WHAT IS THE PROFESSION OF FAITH WE RECITE AT MASS?

The Profession of Faith we recite at Mass is our Creed. It is the Mass prayer in which we declare what we believe.

WHAT IS A FAITH-COMMUNITY?

A faith-community is a community of believers.

WHO ARE THE FAITHFUL?

The faithful are loyal followers of the Lord Jesus.

WHAT IS A NON-BELIEVER?

A non-believer is a person who has not yet received, or has rejected, God's gift of faith.

WHAT IS AN ATHEIST?

An atheist is a person who claims that there is no God or at least he lives as though there were no God.

WHAT IS AN AGNOSTIC?

An agnostic is a person who thinks that we cannot know whether God exists or not.

WHAT IS INDIFFERENTISM?

Indifferentism is the idea that religion is unimportant or the belief that one religion is as good as another.

WHAT IS INFIDELITY?

Infidelity is unfaithfulness, disloyalty.

HOW DOES THE BIBLE SPEAK OF THE PERSON WHO DELIBERATELY CHOOSES TO REJECT GOD?

The Bible speaks of the person who deliberately chooses to reject God as a fool.

The fool says in his heart,
"There is no God" (Ps. 14:1).*

HOW CAN WE HELP TO BRING ATHEISTS TO GOD?

We can help to bring atheists to God by living the way God asks us to live, and by being informed Catholics who are willing to share our knowledge of the Faith with anyone who requests it.

WHAT IS HERESY?

Heresy is the deliberate denial of a truth of faith.

WHAT IS APOSTASY?

Apostasy is complete rejection of the Catholic Faith by a baptized person.

WHAT IS GOD LIKE?

IS GOD PERFECT?

Yes, God is perfect. He is almighty, eternal, all-present, all-good, all-knowing, all-merciful and all-just.

"Nor is he dependent on anything that human hands can do for him, since he can never be in need of anything; on the contrary, it is he who gives everything—including life and breath—to everyone" (Acts 17:25).**

WHAT DO WE MEAN WHEN WE SAY THAT GOD IS ALMIGHTY, ETERNAL, MERCIFUL AND JUST?

Almighty means all-powerful. *Eternal* means "outside of time"—without beginning or end—and unchanging.

> To you, a thousand years are a single day... (Ps. 90:4).**

Merciful means forgiving. *Just* means fair.

WHAT WORD DESCRIBES GOD'S UNLIMITED PERFECTION?

A word that describes God's unlimited perfection is *infinite.* Infinite means perfect, without limitation.

> "...For God everything is possible" (Mt. 19:26).**

DOES GOD CHANGE?

No, God does not change.

> ...With him there is...no shadow of a change (Jas. 1:17).**

WHAT DOES THE NAME "YAHWEH" TELL US ABOUT GOD?

The Old Testament name *Yahweh,* meaning "He who is," tells us that God is life itself.

DOES GOD CARE ABOUT US?

Yes, God cares about us. His loving action in our lives is called divine Providence.

> If I flew to the point of sunrise,
> or westward across the sea,
> your hand would still be guiding me,
> your right hand holding me (Ps. 139:9-10).**

WHAT IS A MYSTERY?

In religion, a mystery is a great truth revealed by God which our limited minds will never be able to wholly understand.

WHAT SPECIAL MYSTERY HAS GOD TOLD US ABOUT HIMSELF?

God has told us about the mystery of the Blessed Trinity. He has revealed Himself to be three Persons in one God—our *triune* God.

WHAT IS THE MYSTERY OF THE BLESSED TRINITY?

The mystery of the Blessed Trinity is one God in three divine Persons—Father, Son and Holy Spirit.

IS THE FATHER GOD?

The Father is God and the First Person of the Blessed Trinity.

IS THE SON GOD?

The Son is God and the Second Person of the Blessed Trinity.

IS THE HOLY SPIRIT GOD?

The Holy Spirit is God and the Third Person of the Blessed Trinity.

CAN WE UNDERSTAND ANYTHING ABOUT THE MYSTERY OF THE BLESSED TRINITY?

We can understand that by "one God" we mean the one divine nature, while by "three Persons" we mean the Father, Son and Holy Spirit, who possess the divine nature.

WHAT IS THE IMPORTANCE OF THE MYSTERY OF THE BLESSED TRINITY FOR OUR OWN LIVES?

The importance of the mystery of the Blessed Trinity for our own lives consists in this: the three Persons of the Trinity call us to everlasting happiness with them. At

Baptism they came to live within us. If we grow in grace through the sacraments and virtuous living, we will draw closer to our Triune God throughout life, and will share eternal union with them in heaven.

GOD OUR CREATOR

WHO IS THE FATHER?

The Father is the First Person of the Blessed Trinity, who is also called the Creator.

In the beginning,...God created the heavens and the earth... (Gn. 1:1).*

WHAT DOES "CREATE" MEAN?

To create means to bring something out of nothing—which only God can do.

WHAT DID GOD CREATE?

God created all the matter and energy in the universe, as well as the pure spirits called angels and the soul of each one of us.

...Not one thing had its being but through him (Jn. 1:3).**

WHY DID GOD CREATE THE WORLD?

God created the world out of His goodness, and to show and share His perfections with us.

WHAT ARE ANGELS?

Angels are spirits, or real spiritual beings, without bodies. They have understanding and free will.

CAN WE PROVE FROM REASON ALONE THAT ANGELS EXIST?

We cannot prove from reason alone that angels exist, yet the existence of angels is not contrary to reason.

It is very "reasonable" to suggest that just as there are creatures composed totally of matter, and creatures made up of matter and spirit, so it is right that there should be purely spiritual creatures.

HOW MANY ANGELS ARE THERE?

The exact number of angels is unknown, but the Bible tells us that there are many. Jesus Himself in the garden of Gethsemane said:

"Do you not suppose I can call on my Father to provide at a moment's notice more than twelve legions of angels?" (Mt. 26:53).* (See also: Dn. 7:10, Heb. 1:14, 2 Pt. 2:11.)

DID GOD BESTOW CERTAIN GIFTS ON THE ANGELS WHEN HE CREATED THEM?

God gave special gifts of supernatural grace, wisdom, power, and holiness to the angels. They were also given the opportunity to merit heaven—the direct vision of God—by remaining faithful to Him.

DID EVERY ANGEL REMAIN FAITHFUL TO GOD?

Not all of the angels remained faithful to God; some sinned. Scripture says:

Did God spare even the angels who sinned? He did not! (2 Pt. 2:4)* (See also: Jude 6.)

WHAT WAS THE REWARD GRANTED TO THE FAITHFUL ANGELS?

The angels who remained faithful to God were admitted to the face-to-face presence of God. These good angels see, love, and adore God eternally, and live intimately with Him.

DO THE GOOD ANGELS HELP US?

The good angels do help us especially by praying for us, by bringing messages from God to us (see: Ex. 23:20, Tob. 5, Lk. 1:28), and by being our guardian angels.

WHO ARE THE GUARDIAN ANGELS?

The guardian angels are pure spirits who watch over us and encourage us to lead good Christian lives.

WHO ARE ARCHANGELS?

Archangels are members of a certain group of angels. From the Bible we know the names of three: Michael, Raphael and Gabriel.

No, the Lord himself will come down from heaven at the word of command, at the sound of the archangel's voice and God's trumpet... (1 Thes. 4:16).*

WHAT HAPPENED TO THE UNFAITHFUL ANGELS?

The unfaithful angels who rebelled against God were sent to hell. They are called devils or evil spirits. Jesus said:

"Out of my sight, you condemned, into that everlasting fire prepared for the devil and his angels!" (Mt. 25:41)**

DO THE UNFAITHFUL ANGELS TRY TO HARM US?

The unfaithful angels do try to harm us chiefly by tempting us to sin. Says Scripture:

Stay sober and alert. Your opponent the devil is prowling like a roaring lion looking for someone to devour. Resist him, solid in your faith, realizing that the brotherhood of believers is undergoing the same sufferings throughout the world (1 Pt. 5:8-9).* (See: Mt. 10:1, Eph. 6:11.)

DO ALL OF OUR TEMPTATIONS TO SIN COME FROM THE UNFAITHFUL ANGELS?

All of our temptations to sin do not come from the unfaithful angels, but some of them do. Other temptations come from ourselves—our wounded human nature—and from the persons and things about us. Scripture says:

My inner self agrees with the law of God, but I see in my body's members another law at war with the law of my mind; this makes me the prisoner of the law of sin in my members (Rom. 7:22-23).* (See also: Jas. 1:13-14, 1 Jn. 2:15.)

ARE WE HUMAN BEINGS ALWAYS ABLE TO RESIST ALL TEMPTATIONS?

We human beings are always able to resist all temptations, because temptations—no matter how powerful—are not sins in themselves, and because God will always give us His grace and strength if we ask Him. St. Paul said:

For all these reasons, let anyone who thinks he is standing upright watch out lest he fall! No test has been sent you that does not come to all men. Besides, God keeps his promise. He will not let you be tested beyond your strength (1 Cor. 10:12-13).*

WHAT IS A HUMAN BEING?

A human being is a creature with a material body and a soul that will live forever. The Bible says:

He (God) himself made man in the beginning,
     and then left him free to make his own decisions
(Sir. 15:14).**

WHO WERE THE FIRST MAN AND WOMAN?

The first man and woman were Adam and Eve, the first parents of the entire human race. (See Genesis, chapters 1-4.)

WHAT WAS THE MOST IMPORTANT GIFT GIVEN TO OUR FIRST PARENTS BY GOD?

The most important gift given to our first parents by God was sanctifying grace.

WHAT OTHER GIFTS DID OUR FIRST PARENTS RECEIVE FROM GOD?

Other gifts our first parents received from God were: natural happiness, knowledge, passions controlled by reason, and freedom from suffering and death.

WERE ADAM AND EVE CAPABLE OF SINNING?

Adam and Eve were capable of sinning because God had given them a free will.

WHAT DOES IT MEAN TO SIN?

To sin means to purposely disobey God's Law and will. (Personal sin: see page 134ff.)

DID ADAM AND EVE SIN?

Yes, Adam and Eve did sin.

The woman saw that the tree was good for food, pleasing to the eyes, and desirable for gaining wisdom. So she took some of its fruit and ate it; and she also gave some to her husband, who was with her, and he ate it (Gen. 3:6).*

WHAT HAPPENED TO OUR FIRST PARENTS BECAUSE OF THEIR SIN?

Because of their sin our first parents lost sanctifying grace, the right to heaven, and the gifts they had received. They became subject to suffering and death, felt strong inclinations to evil, and were driven from the garden of paradise.

DOES THE SIN OF OUR FIRST PARENTS HAVE ANY EFFECT ON US, THE DESCENDENTS OF ADAM?

The sin of our first parents does affect us, the descendents of Adam. Because of it, we are born without sanctifying grace and inherit Adam's punishment as we would have inherited his gifts had he been faithful to God.

WHAT IS THIS SIN IN US CALLED?

This sin in us is called original sin.

HOW CAN ORIGINAL SIN BEST BE DESCRIBED?

Original sin can best be described as the lack of grace with which each of us comes into the world, because our first parents lost grace both for themselves and for us. (Grace: see page 55ff.)

WAS ANYONE EVER FREE FROM ORIGINAL SIN?

Yes, Mary, Jesus' Mother, in view of the merits of her divine Son, was preserved from original sin from the moment of her conception in the womb of St. Anne. This great privilege is called the Immaculate Conception. It was proclaimed a dogma of faith by Pope Pius IX in 1854, and is celebrated every year on December 8.

AFTER CREATING US, DOES GOD LEAVE US ON OUR OWN?

After creating us, God does not leave us on our own. Without His activity in our lives we could not think, decide or act. In fact, God actually keeps the whole universe from returning to nothingness (See 2 Mc. 7:28).

WHAT ARE THE MAIN FACTS TO KNOW ABOUT CREATION?

The main facts to know about creation are: all matter and energy in the universe were created by God. If there *was* evolution, God planned and guided it. Every human soul is created directly by God at the moment of the conception of the body.

HOW SHOULD WE THINK OF CREATION?

We should think of creation as just the beginning of all of God's saving actions in the world and in our own lives.

WHAT IS THE GREATEST GLORY THAT GOD RECEIVES IN THE VISIBLE UNIVERSE?

The greatest glory that God receives in the visible universe comes from human beings because only human beings have a free will to choose to love, adore and serve Him. The most perfect way that we can cooperate with God in this life is to become holy, that is to do His will as perfectly as we can ourselves, and bring other people to Him.

WHAT IS THE THEORY OF EVOLUTION?

The theory of evolution is development through change, often used in reference to the development of the universe, plants, animals and man. Our Catholic Faith teaches that even if it should ever be proven that the human body formed through a process of evolution, still each and every human soul is created directly by God.

WHAT IS SALVATION HISTORY?

Salvation history is the history of God's frequent actions in the lives of human beings to free them from sin and to bring them to Himself.

DO WE OURSELVES HAVE A PART IN SALVATION HISTORY?

We ourselves do have a part in salvation history and should cooperate with God in making His creation give Him the glory and praise He deserves. We do this by sharing in His life of grace made available to us through His Church.

WHAT ARE THE GREATEST OF GOD'S SAVING ACTIONS?

The greatest of God's saving actions are the incarnation, death and resurrection of Jesus, His only-begotten Son.

WHY ARE WE ON THIS EARTH?

WHAT IS THE PURPOSE OF OUR LIFE ON EARTH?

The purpose of our life on earth is to attain happiness—the everlasting happiness that we can find only in God.

Man has life and death before him;
whichever a man likes better will be given him
(Sir. 15:17-18).**

WHY IS IT THAT ONLY GOD CAN MAKE US HAPPY?

Only God can make us happy because He gave us such a great desire for happiness that nothing less than union with Him can satisfy us.

WILL THIS HAPPINESS COME TO US AUTOMATICALLY?

This happiness will not come to us automatically. Because our eternal destiny is so great, God asks us to *earn* it with His help. We *can* earn it by knowing, loving and serving Him.

Work for your salvation in "fear and trembling" (Phil. 2:12).**

HOW CAN WE KNOW GOD?

We can know God by studying about Him and believing what we have learned. In religion, to *believe* means to be sure about.

HOW CAN WE LOVE AND SERVE GOD?

We can love and serve God mainly by:

— *wanting* to love and serve Him
— avoiding sin
— sharing in the sacramental life, especially the frequent reception of Penance and Eucharist
— remaining loyal to the teachings and laws of Christ's Church
— drawing others to Him by living a Christ-like life.

WHEN CAN WE SHARE IN GOD'S HAPPINESS?

We can *begin* to share in God's happiness even now, by living good lives, which bring peace of heart. But by far the greatest happiness will be enjoyed after death. It is then that the faithful person will hear:

"Well done, good and faithful servant.... Come and join in your master's happiness" (Mt. 25:23).**

DOES EVERY HUMAN BEING LIVE ON AFTER DEATH?

The human soul is immortal. After the resurrection from the dead, body and soul will be reunited to live on forever after death.

"Those who have done right shall rise to live;
the evildoers shall rise to be damned" (Jn. 5:29).*

WHAT DO WE CALL THE PLACE OR CONDITION OF EVERLASTING HAPPINESS WITH GOD?

The place or condition of everlasting happiness with God is called heaven.

HOW DO WE KNOW THAT THERE IS A HEAVEN?

We know that there is a heaven because God Himself has told us. Jesus spoke many times of the eternal reward that awaits the just.

"Then the saints will shine like the sun in their Father's kingdom. Let everyone heed what he hears!" (Mt. 13:43)*

IS IT IMPORTANT TO KEEP HEAVEN IN MIND?

It *is* important to keep heaven in mind, because this thought helps us to lead better lives, and to be happier because we look forward to being eternally with God. It also helps us to do more good with our lives.

...The more you sow, the more you reap.... *God loves a cheerful giver.* And there is no limit to the blessings which God can send you (2 Cor. 9:6-8).**

WHAT SHOULD THE THOUGHT OF HEAVEN DO FOR US?

The thought of heaven should make us more eager to work and to help others, for God wants this and will reward all the good we do. Jesus said:

"Your light must shine in the sight of men, so that, seeing your good works, they may give the praise to your Father in heaven" (Mt. 5:16).**

DOES OUR SALVATION MEAN MUCH TO GOD?

Our salvation does mean much to God. St. Paul said:

With God on our side who can be against us? Since God did not spare his own Son, but gave him up to benefit us all, we may be certain, after such a gift, that he will not refuse anything he can give (Rom. 8:31-32).**

GOD SENDS HIS SON

WHERE DO WE LEARN ABOUT GOD'S REVELATION?

We learn about God's revelation in Sacred Scripture (the Bible), and Sacred Tradition, as taught to us by the teaching authority of the Church.

WHAT IS THE BIBLE?

The Bible is God's own word, written down by men who were guided by the Holy Spirit. It is our Father's letter to us.

WHAT ARE THE MAIN PARTS OF THE BIBLE?

The main parts of the Bible are the Old Testament and New Testament.

HOW IS THE BIBLE DIVIDED?

The Bible is divided into the 46 books of the Old Testament (written before the birth of Jesus) and the 27 books of the New Testament (written after Jesus' resurrection).

WHAT IS THE BIBLE'S MAIN THEME?

The Bible's main theme is God's saving love for us human beings, even though we are sinful.

WHAT IS THE BIBLE ALSO CALLED?

The Bible is also called Sacred Scripture, the Scriptures, or the Word of God.

WHAT DO WE MEAN WHEN WE SAY THAT THE BIBLE WAS WRITTEN UNDER DIVINE INSPIRATION?

When we say that the Bible was written under divine inspiration, we mean the special guidance that the Holy Spirit gave to the Bible's human authors, so that they wrote everything God wanted them to write and only that.

All scripture is inspired by God and can profitably be used for teaching, for refuting error, for guiding people's lives and teaching them to be holy (2 Tim. 3:16).**

WHAT IS THE OLD TESTAMENT ABOUT?

The Old Testament tells the history of God's saving actions in the lives of the "chosen people"—the Hebrew or Jewish people—actions which prepared them and the world for the coming of the Savior.

BRIEFLY, WHAT IS THE HISTORY OF THE CHOSEN PEOPLE?

Briefly, the history of the chosen people began when God called Abraham to be the father of the chosen people. He called Moses to free His people from slavery in Egypt and gave them the ten commandments. He chose Joshua to lead His people into the "Promised Land"—Canaan. He chose David to be a great king of His people and an ancestor of Christ. He chose prophets (spokesmen), such as Isaiah and Jeremiah to urge His people to obey His law. Several of the prophets also foretold the coming of Christ.

At one point, God permitted the destruction of the center of worship, Jerusalem, and the exile of its people into Babylon. The exiles who returned to Jerusalem were, on the whole, more religious than their ancestors and more obedient to God's law. Thus, they were more ready for the coming of Christ.

WHAT IS THE NEW TESTAMENT ABOUT?

The New Testament is about the birth, life, teachings, death and resurrection of Jesus Christ, the Son of God, as well as the life and growth of the early Church which He founded.

WHAT DO WE LEARN FROM THE GOSPELS?

From the Gospels we learn what Jesus asks us to believe and do in order to be saved and reach heaven. We learn about the great love of Jesus and His Father for us. Because of this love, Jesus died for us, to repair for our sins.

WHO ARE THE HUMAN AUTHORS OF THE FOUR GOSPELS?

The human authors of the four Gospels, called evangelists (Gospel writers), are Matthew, Mark, Luke and John. They were inspired by the Holy Spirit, so they wrote only what was true.

CAN PEOPLE MAKE MISTAKES WHEN THEY TRY TO UNDERSTAND THE BIBLE?

People can make mistakes when they try to understand the Bible; one of the reasons Jesus gave us the Church is to explain the Bible to us. (Church: see page 61ff.)

WHAT IS DIVINE OR SACRED TRADITION?

Divine or sacred Tradition is the teachings of Jesus or of the apostles illumined by the Holy Spirit that were not written by the first Christians but passed on from the apostles through their successors. Tradition was later written down, mainly in the official teachings of the Church.

There were many other signs that Jesus worked and the disciples saw, but they are not recorded in this book (Jn. 20:30).**

HOW IMPORTANT IS DIVINE TRADITION?

Divine or sacred Tradition is just as important as the Bible, because it, too, is part of God's revelation.

Stand firm,...brothers, and keep the traditions that we taught you, whether by word of mouth or by letter (2 Thes. 2:15).**

WHY DOES THE CHURCH EXPLAIN THE BIBLE AND TRADITION TO US?

The Church explains the Bible and Tradition so we will be sure about what Jesus wants us to believe and do, since the Church has special help from God.

WHEN DID SALVATION HISTORY START?

Salvation history started at the time of our first parents, who sinned seriously and lost God's grace for themselves and their descendants. Sin began to spread in the world, but God did not leave the human race. He offered a covenant to man again and again. Through the prophets He taught man to hope for salvation. When the right time had come, He sent His Son to die for our sins and give us the chance of obtaining the happiness of heaven.

Now, by the working of the Holy Spirit, God continues to bring to all men the salvation that Jesus won for us on Calvary's cross.

WHO IS THE SAVIOR OF ALL PEOPLE?

The Savior of all people is Jesus.

WHO IS JESUS CHRIST?

Jesus Christ is God the Son, the second Person of the Blessed Trinity, who became man to save us.

...When the designated time had come, God sent forth his Son born of a woman...so that we might receive our status as adopted sons (Gal. 4:4-5).*

IS JESUS TRULY GOD AND TRULY MAN?

Jesus is truly God and truly man.

WHAT IS MEANT BY HYPOSTATIC UNION?

Hypostatic union is a term used to describe the union of Jesus' divine nature and His human nature in one Person—the second Person of the Blessed Trinity.

WAS JESUS ALWAYS GOD AND ALWAYS MAN?

Jesus was always God, but He was not always man. The name we give to His taking of a human body and soul is the *Incarnation.*

Jesus will remain both God and man forever.

WHAT CAN WE UNDERSTAND ABOUT JESUS' BEING BOTH GOD AND MAN?

Jesus is only one Person, and that Person is God the Son. Because He has two natures—God's nature and a human nature—He is both God and man.

WHAT DO WE MEAN BY NATURE AND PERSON?

A *nature* is *what* something or someone is. A *person* is *who* someone is. Jesus is one Person with two natures. This is a great mystery of our Faith.

IS JESUS STILL BOTH GOD AND MAN?

Yes, Jesus is still both God and man and will continue to be so forever.

WHY DID THE SON OF GOD BECOME MAN?

The Son of God became man to teach us what to believe, to show us the right way to live, and above all to die and rise for our salvation.

[God]...has spoken to us through his Son... (Heb. 1:2).*

WHO WAS JESUS' MOTHER?

Jesus' Mother was the Blessed Virgin Mary, a Jewish girl from Nazareth. Tradition tells us that her parents were Saints Joachim and Ann.

WHO IS JESUS' FATHER?

Jesus' Father is God the Father.

WHO WAS SAINT JOSEPH?

St. Joseph was Jesus' foster father and His guardian.

AT WHAT MOMENT DID THE SON OF GOD BECOME A MAN?

The Son of God became a man at the moment in which Mary agreed to become His Mother; the second Person of the Blessed Trinity took a human body and soul in her womb, through the power of the Holy Spirit.

WHAT IS MEANT BY THE ANNUNCIATION?

By the Annunciation is meant the day (usually March 25) on which the Church recalls the Angel Gabriel's announcement to Mary, her acceptance, and the Incarnation of the Son.

IS MARY REALLY THE MOTHER OF GOD?

Yes, Mary is really the Mother of God, because she is the Mother of Jesus who is God.

WHAT IS MEANT BY THE VIRGIN-BIRTH?

By the virgin-birth is meant that our Lady remained a virgin before, during and after the birth of Christ.

WHAT DOES THE NAME JESUS CHRIST MEAN?

The name Jesus means "God saves," or "the Savior." Christ means "the Messiah."

WHERE WAS JESUS BORN?

Jesus was born in Bethlehem of Judea, the small town in which King David was born.

WHAT DOES THE WORD *SAVIOR* MEAN?

A savior is one who saves, that is, who frees people from sin and brings them to God. The "Messiah" was the great leader foretold in the Old Testament who would set up God's kingdom on earth.

"...You are to name him Jesus because he will save his people from their sins" (Mt. 1:21).*

HOW DID JESUS SHOW US HOW TO LIVE?

Jesus showed us how to live especially by His examples, that is, by the way He lived His private and public life. His public life is His life of teaching; it probably lasted a little over two years. The public life ended with Jesus' death and resurrection.

WHERE DO WE ESPECIALLY LEARN ABOUT THE LIFE AND TEACHINGS OF JESUS?

We especially learn about the life and teachings of Jesus from the four Gospels.

DO THE GOSPELS SHOW THAT JESUS IS TRULY GOD?

Yes, the Gospels show that Jesus is truly God. In ways that were very clear for the people of His time and country, Jesus showed that He was God. For example, Jesus said:

"Everything has been given over to me by my Father. No one knows the Son but the Father, and no one knows the Father but the Son—and anyone to whom the Son wishes to reveal him" (Mt. 11:27).*

HOW DID JESUS BACK UP HIS CLAIM TO BE GOD?

Jesus backed up His claim to be God by working miracles and prophesying.

"...The works my Father has given me to carry out,
these same works of mine
testify that the Father has sent me" (Jn. 5:36).**

WHAT IS A MIRACLE?

A miracle is something that takes place outside of the ordinary working of nature's laws—something only God can do, because He made the laws.

WHAT IS PROPHECY?

Prophecy may be concerned with future events, but it is basically the mediation and interpretation of the divine mind and will.

DO THE GOSPELS SHOW THAT JESUS WAS TRULY MAN?

Yes, the Gospels do show that Jesus was truly man. From the Gospels we can see that Jesus grew from infancy to manhood and that He was hungry, thirsty and tired as we also become. In the garden of Gethsemane, He prayed for His Father's will, not His own, to be done—which showed that He had a human will distinct from His divine will. These are only some of the Gospel examples that prove how human Jesus was.

JESUS WAS CALLED MASTER OR TEACHER. WHOM DID HE TEACH?

Jesus taught everyone who came to listen to Him, but He gave special training to His disciples, especially the twelve Apostles.

WHAT WAS JESUS' GREATEST MIRACLE?

Jesus' greatest miracle was His resurrection. When the apostle Thomas saw the risen Jesus, he adored Him as God. Jesus let him do this, which again shows that He was divine.

WHAT WERE SOME OF JESUS' PROPHECIES?

Jesus prophesied His passion and resurrection, His denial by Peter, His betrayal by Judas, and the destruction of the temple (which took place about forty years after His Ascension).

WHY DO JESUS' MIRACLES AND PROPHECIES PROVE THAT HE IS DIVINE?

The miracles and prophecies of Jesus could only have been done if God was with Him and thus approved what He had said about being divine.

THE MEN WHO FOLLOWED JESUS IN A SPECIAL WAY WERE CALLED DISCIPLES OR APOSTLES. WHAT DO THESE WORDS MEAN?

Disciple means learner or follower; *apostle* means "one who is sent." Jesus had been sent into the world by His Father; now He was preparing to send His apostles into the world as His messengers.

WHAT IS THE REDEMPTION?

The redemption is the ransom or rescue of all of us by Jesus, who laid down His life for us.

"The Son of Man has not come to be served but to serve —to give his life in ransom for the many" (Mk. 10:45).*

WHY DID JESUS DIE?

Jesus died to make up for the great offenses of our first parents' sin and our own personal sins. But, more than that, He died so that we might receive God's life called grace, and have a chance of reaching the happiness of heaven.

DID JESUS HAVE TO SUFFER AND DIE TO SAVE US?

No, Jesus did not have to suffer and die to save us. He freely chose to do so.

"I am the good shepherd;
the good shepherd lays down his life for the sheep" (Jn. 10:11).*

WHAT DO WE LEARN FROM JESUS' CHOICE OF DEATH FOR OUR SAKE?

Jesus' choice of death for our sake teaches us how much He loves us and how terrible sin is.

"A man can have no greater love
than to lay down his life for his friends" (Jn. 15:13).**

WAS GOD "OBLIGED" TO GIVE US A SECOND CHANCE AFTER THE SIN OF OUR FIRST PARENTS?

God was not "obliged" to give mankind a "second chance" for heaven after the sin of our first parents. But He chose to do so, and at the cost of His Son's life. All of us are responsible for Jesus' death; we cannot put the blame on particular individuals or groups.

...Jesus was to die for the nation—and not for the nation only, but to gather together in unity the scattered children of God (Jn. 11:51-52).**

DID JESUS DIE FOR ALL MEN?

Yes, Jesus died for all men; He is our Redeemer.
He is an offering for our sins,
and not for our sins only,
but for those of the whole world (1 Jn. 2:2).*

DID JESUS REALLY DIE?

Jesus really did die.

...I taught you...that Christ died for our sins...that he was buried; and that he was raised to life on the third day... (1 Cor. 15:3-4).**

This means that His human soul separated from His human body.

To remove any doubt, the Gospels tell us clearly that Jesus was already dead when the soldier pierced His heart with a lance.

WHAT DO WE CALL THE SUFFERINGS OF JESUS BEFORE HIS DEATH?

The sufferings of Jesus before His death are called His *passion.*

WHAT IS GOOD FRIDAY?

Good Friday is the Friday before Easter, on which we remember in a special way our Savior's sufferings and death for us on Calvary.

DID JESUS TRULY RISE TO LIFE AGAIN?

Jesus did truly rise to life again as the Gospels clearly tell us. The reunion of Jesus' body and soul was brought about by God's power, which the Father, Son and Holy Spirit each possess.

WHAT IS JESUS' RISING FROM THE DEAD CALLED?

Jesus' rising from the dead is called His *resurrection.*

WHY IS THE RESURRECTION OF JESUS IMPORTANT?

The resurrection of Jesus is important because it shows that He truly is God as He said and, therefore, that His death really saved us. St. Paul said:

...Christ, as we know, having been raised from the dead will never die again. Death has no power over him any more (Rom. 6:9).**

WHAT DO WE CALL THE PASSION, DEATH AND RESURRECTION OF JESUS?

The passion, death and resurrection of Jesus are called the *paschal mystery.* "Paschal" is a word that refers to Passover and Easter; "mystery" here means event. (The Ascension may also be considered part of the paschal mystery.)

WHAT DOES JESUS' RESURRECTION TELL US ABOUT OUR OWN FUTURE RESURRECTION?

Jesus' resurrection also shows us what our own resurrection will be like at the end of the world. Just as God's power united Jesus' body and soul, so will our own bodies and souls be reunited by God's power at the end of time.

WHAT FOLLOWED JESUS' RESURRECTION?

After His resurrection, Jesus appeared to His followers a number of times to show that He had truly risen and to prepare them for their mission. Then He ascended to His Father.

He had shown himself alive to them after his Passion by many demonstrations... (Acts 1:3).**

WHAT IS JESUS' VISIBLE DEPARTURE FROM THIS WORLD CALLED?

Jesus' visible departure from the world is called the *Ascension.* This important event is commemorated each year on Ascension Thursday, forty days after Easter.

IS JESUS PRESENT IN OUR WORLD TODAY?

Yes, Jesus is present in our world today. He is completely present (as both God and man) in the Eucharist. He is also present in the other sacraments, His actions that give us the Holy Spirit and grace. Also, by His power as God, He speaks to us through the Bible and the Church, especially the Pope.

"I BELIEVE IN THE HOLY SPIRIT..."

WHO IS THE HOLY SPIRIT?

The Holy Spirit is the Third Person of the Blessed Trinity.

You...have been stamped with the seal of the Holy Spirit of the Promise... (Eph 1:13).** (See also: Rom. 8:14, 17; Acts 1:8.)

IS THE HOLY SPIRIT GOD?

The Holy Spirit is God as is the Father and the Son.

WHAT ARE SOME OTHER NAMES FOR THE HOLY SPIRIT?

Some other names for the Holy Spirit are: Spirit of God, Gift of God, Spirit of Truth, Giver of Life and Paraclete.

WHAT DOES "PARACLETE" MEAN?

Paraclete means "someone called upon for help." The term is especially used in relationship to a court of law. Jesus explained to the apostles that the Holy Spirit, the Paraclete, would prosecute the world. At the Last Supper, Jesus said:

"When he (the Paraclete) comes,
he will prove the world wrong
about sin,
about justice,
about condemnation" (Jn. 16:8).*

WHAT DOES THE HOLY SPIRIT DO FOR US?

The Holy Spirit transforms us through grace, the virtues, His gifts and actual graces. He helps us to know Jesus, our Savior, and our Father in heaven. He helps us to pray and to evangelize.

WHAT DOES THE HOLY SPIRIT DO FOR THE CHURCH?

The Holy Spirit joins God's people, the Church, in faith and love. He guides the Church's chief teachers—the Pope and bishops united to the Pope—so that they will not make mistakes. He gives us the grace Jesus won for us by His death on the cross.

WHEN DID THE HOLY SPIRIT FIRST MAKE HIMSELF KNOWN TO JESUS' FOLLOWERS?

Although the Holy Spirit was active in the world before Jesus' resurrection, we think of Pentecost as the day when He first made Himself known to Jesus' followers. He gave the Apostles courage, a deeper understanding of Jesus' teachings, and a spirit of sacrifice. He gave them grace and joined them more closely together.

"Surely we cannot help speaking of what we have heard and seen" (Acts 4:20).*

WHAT IS THE SPECIAL GIFT THAT THE HOLY SPIRIT GIVES US?

The special gift that the Holy Spirit gives us is *grace* which was won for us by Jesus' death on the cross.

Jesus died and rose, not only to make up for the great offense of our sins, but also to give us a chance to reach heaven through grace.

IN GENERAL, WHAT IS GRACE?

Grace, God's divine life in us, is a special gift which He freely gives us so that we may share in His happiness. Grace means "loving favor." God's grace is supernatural—that is, "above the powers of any creature." Thus, grace brings us close to God.

ARE THERE DIFFERENT KINDS OF GRACE?

There are two kinds of grace: sanctifying and actual. *(Both terms will be explained below.)*

WHY ARE THERE DIFFERENT KINDS OF GRACE?

There are different kinds of grace because we need many kinds of help from God, and He is generous in giving this help.

WHAT IS THE "STATE OF GRACE"?

The state of grace is a sharing in God's own life—a state of friendship with Him.

HOW ELSE MAY WE REFER TO OUR "SHARING IN GOD'S LIFE"?

This sharing in God's own life may also be called *sanctifying grace,* which means a divine gift that makes us holy. This grace is necessary for sharing in God's life and happiness after death.

WHAT DOES A PERSON IN THE STATE OF GRACE BECOME?

A person in the state of grace becomes an adopted son or daughter of the Father. The three Persons of the

Blessed Trinity live in this person as in a "temple." St. Paul says:

Are you not aware that you are the temple of God, and that the Spirit of God dwells in you? (1 Cor. 3:16)* (See also: Jn. 14:16-17; 14:23.)

WHAT IS MERIT?

Merit is the "right" to a reward in heaven earned by those who have God's grace and pray or do good works for love of Him.

WHAT IS SANCTIFYING GRACE?

Sanctifying grace is the gift of God which gives us a share in His own life and makes us holy. When we possess sanctifying grace, it may be said that we are in the *state of grace.*

WHAT CAN DRIVE SANCTIFYING GRACE FROM OUR SOULS?

Mortal sin can drive sanctifying grace from our souls.

WHAT ARE ACTUAL GRACES?

Actual graces are temporary helps from the Holy Spirit which make us able to know and do what God expects of us at a certain moment. Actual grace may also be described as a temporary light for the mind or strength for the will by which God helps us to avoid sin or to do something good.

WHAT DOES "LIGHT FOR THE MIND" MEAN?

Light for the mind means a good thought or a clearer understanding of what God expects or invites us to do here and now.

ARE ACTUAL GRACES DIFFERENT FROM THE VIRTUES AND GIFTS?

Actual graces are different from the virtues and gifts, inasmuch as they are temporary, whereas the virtues and gifts are "permanent" in the soul. (In fact, some of the virtues remain even when grace has been driven from the soul by mortal sin.)

TO WHOM DOES GOD GIVE ACTUAL GRACES?

God gives actual graces to everyone.

HOW POWERFUL ARE ACTUAL GRACES?

Actual graces do not force us to do what is right, because God leaves us free. Actual graces are powerful if we cooperate with them.

WHAT IS A VIRTUE?

A virtue is a power to do good or a habit of doing good.

The main God-given virtues are the theological (God-centered) virtues and cardinal (hinge or key) virtues. Although these powers are free gifts of God, we must use them, so that they truly become the habits of doing good that God meant them to be.

WHAT ARE THE THEOLOGICAL VIRTUES?

The theological virtues are God-given and God-centered habits of doing good—by name: faith, hope and charity.

WHAT DO WE MEAN BY THE WORD "THEOLOGICAL"?

By the word "theological" is meant: that which pertains to God.

WHAT IS THE VIRTUE OF FAITH?

Faith is the virtue by which we believe in God and everything He has taught us.

WHAT DOES THE VIRTUE OF FAITH DO FOR US?

St. Peter says that the virtue of faith does this for us:

You did not see him, yet you love him; and still without seeing him, you are already filled with a joy so glorious that it cannot be described, because you believe... (1 Pt. 1:8).**

WHAT IS THE VIRTUE OF HOPE?

Hope is the virtue by which we trust that our all-powerful and faithful God will bring us to heaven if we live as He asks us to live.

WHAT IS THE VIRTUE OF CHARITY?

Charity is the virtue by which we love God above everything else and love all other people for His sake.

Jesus said, "You must love the Lord your God with all your heart, with all your soul, and with all your mind. This is the greatest and the first commandment. The second resembles it: You must love your neighbor as yourself" (Mt. 22:37-39).**

WHAT ARE THE ACTS OF FAITH, HOPE AND LOVE (CHARITY)?

The acts of faith, hope and love (charity) are prayers that express our belief, our trust, and our love for God.

WHAT VIRTUES ARE CALLED "CARDINAL"?

The cardinal virtues are prudence, justice, fortitude and temperance.

WHY ARE THESE VIRTUES CALLED *CARDINAL?*
These virtues are called *cardinal* because they are four "key" or "hinge" virtues on which all the other virtues about right living (moral virtues) depend.

WHAT IS THE VIRTUE OF PRUDENCE?
Prudence is the virtue by which a person puts heaven before everything else, thinks carefully before acting, makes wise choices, and does things well.

WHAT IS THE VIRTUE OF JUSTICE?
Justice is the virtue by which a person is fair to everyone—first of all, to God.

WHAT IS THE VIRTUE OF FORTITUDE?
Fortitude is the virtue by which a person does what is good and right in spite of any difficulty.

WHAT IS THE VIRTUE OF TEMPERANCE?
Temperance is the virtue by which a person exercises self-control with regard to the drives of human nature.

WHAT IS MEANT BY THE GIFTS OF THE HOLY SPIRIT?
The gifts of the Holy Spirit are seven special inclinations that the Spirit gives us so that we will be more ready and willing to do what He expects of us. The gifts of the Holy Spirit prepare us to receive actual graces and make it easier to practice the virtues.

WHAT ARE THE GIFTS OF THE HOLY SPIRIT?
The gifts of the Holy Spirit are wisdom, understanding, right judgment (or counsel), courage (or fortitude), knowledge, reverent love (or piety) and holy fear.

WHAT IS THE GIFT OF WISDOM?

Wisdom is the gift which helps us to love spiritual things, to put God in the first place in our lives, and to look at everything either as a help or an obstacle to reaching heaven.

WHAT IS THE GIFT OF UNDERSTANDING?

The gift of understanding helps us to see more deeply into the truths we already believe by faith.

WHAT IS THE GIFT OF RIGHT JUDGMENT?

Right judgment helps us to choose what is right, even in difficult circumstances.

WHAT IS THE GIFT OF COURAGE?

Courage is the gift which helps us to be brave and patient in overcoming difficulties and carrying out our duties.

WHAT IS THE GIFT OF KNOWLEDGE?

Knowledge is the gift which helps us to know God and what He expects of us through what He has created.

WHAT IS THE GIFT OF REVERENT LOVE?

Reverent love helps us to love God as our Father and all people as our brothers and sisters, so that we will serve both Him and them.

WHAT IS THE GIFT OF HOLY FEAR?

Holy fear helps us to respect God and to want to please Him in everything.

WHAT ARE THE FRUITS OF THE HOLY SPIRIT?

The fruits of the Holy Spirit are good deeds and habits that result from our response to the Holy Spirit's impulses to do good (actual graces). The gifts are: charity, joy, peace, patience, kindness, goodness, long-suffering, humility, fidelity, modesty, continence, chastity.

WHAT IS HUMILITY?

Humility is the virtue by which we truly know ourselves and see that whatever is good in us comes from God.

"I BELIEVE IN THE HOLY CATHOLIC CHURCH..."

WHAT DO WE CALL THE CHURCH FOUNDED BY JESUS?

We call the Church founded by Jesus the Catholic Church.

WHAT IS THE CATHOLIC CHURCH?

The Catholic Church is the true Church founded by Jesus Christ, which can be known by these characteristics together: loyalty to the Pope and bishops joined with him; oneness in the truths to be believed and the moral code to be followed; oneness in worship: the Sacrifice of the Mass, and the means to holiness, the seven sacraments.

WHY DID JESUS START HIS CHURCH?

Jesus started His Church to continue His mission of bringing all men to eternal salvation. St. Peter told the first Christians:

You are the People of God... (1 Pt. 2:10).**

WHAT SPECIAL ROLE DOES THE HOLY SPIRIT HAVE IN THE LIFE OF THE CHURCH?

The Holy Spirit's special role in the Church is to keep its members faithful to Jesus' teachings until the end of time. The Holy Spirit also helps the Church to constantly become holier and better in the Church itself and in its members.

The Church of the living God...upholds the truth and keeps it safe (1 Tim. 3:15).**

WHAT ARE THE FOUR CHARACTERISTICS BY WHICH WE IDENTIFY THE TRUE CHURCH IN OUR WORLD TODAY?

The true Church founded by Christ is one, holy, universal (or catholic) and apostolic. Only the Roman Catholic Church has these four characteristics.

HOW IS THE CATHOLIC CHURCH ONE?

The Catholic Church is one in doctrine (truths of Faith and moral code), in worship, and in government. All Catholics are united through their bishops to the Pope.

There is one Body, one Spirit, just as you were all called into one and the same hope when you were called. There is one Lord, one faith, one baptism... (Eph. 4:4-5).**

HOW IS THE CATHOLIC CHURCH HOLY?

The Catholic Church is holy because her Founder and His doctrine are holy; because her Source of supernatural life, the Holy Spirit, is holy, and because her sacraments give grace which makes people holy.

HOW IS THE CATHOLIC CHURCH CATHOLIC OR UNIVERSAL?

The Catholic Church is catholic or universal because it is meant for all people of all places.

HOW IS THE CATHOLIC CHURCH APOSTOLIC?

The Catholic Church is apostolic because it can be traced back in its foundation to the apostles.

WHAT DO WE MEAN BY THE CATHOLIC FAITH?

By the Catholic Faith we mean the teachings of the Catholic Church; that which we believe.

WHAT CAN WE LEARN FROM THE HISTORY OF THE CHURCH?

From the history of the Church we can learn that Jesus is with His Church, as He promised, no matter how much the Church is persecuted; that the Church has always tried to help all mankind; and that there have been saints in every period for God's people to imitate.

WHAT DO WE MEAN WHEN WE CALL THE CATHOLIC CHURCH *CHRIST'S MYSTICAL BODY?*

When we call the Catholic Church Christ's Mystical Body we mean the real union of members of the Church (living and deceased) with Jesus and one another, through the grace-giving activity of the Holy Spirit. St. Paul said:

...We, though many, are one body in Christ and individually members one of another (Rom. 12:5).* (See also: 1 Cor. 12:27.)

WHAT IS THE POPE'S ROLE IN THE CHURCH?

The Pope is the Vicar of Christ and the chief teacher and leader of God's people. Jesus said:

"...You are Peter and on this rock I will build my Church" (Mt. 16:18).** (See also: Jn. 21:17.)

WHY IS THE POPE SO IMPORTANT TO THE CHURCH?

The Pope is so important to the Church because he is the chief teacher and leader. He is Christ's Vicar. In other words, he holds the place of Jesus in the Church. The Catholic Church will always have a Pope because this is what Jesus wanted.

WHAT DO WE MEAN BY THE PRIMACY OF THE POPE?

By the primacy of the Pope is meant the "first place" that the Pope holds in the Church in teaching, governing and guiding Catholics in what they believe and in how they live.

WHAT DO WE MEAN BY THE TITLE: "PRINCE OF THE APOSTLES"?

The title "Prince of the Apostles" was given to St. Peter, the first Pope. It means that he is the *first* among the apostles; the leader of the group.

WHY IS IT IMPORTANT TO FOLLOW THE POPE?

It is important to follow the Pope because the Holy Spirit guides him in teaching us what to believe and do in order to be saved.

WHAT IS MEANT BY THE WORDS "PAPAL" AND "PONTIFF"?

By the word "papal" is meant that which refers to the Pope. "Pontiff," in ordinary speech, is another name for Pope.

WHAT DO WE MEAN WHEN WE SAY THAT THE CATHOLIC CHURCH HAS THE GIFT OF INFALLIBILITY?

The gift of infallibility is freedom from making a mistake when teaching a truth of faith or right living. It comes from the Holy Spirit and is given in certain circumstances to the Pope and the bishops united with him.

WHAT DO WE MEAN BY THE TERM "EX CATHEDRA"?

The term "ex cathedra" is Latin and it means "from the chair" of St. Peter. It is used when referring to the Pope's infallible statements regarding what Catholics must believe and live.

WHAT IS VATICAN CITY?

Vatican City is the city (which is also an independent nation) in which the Pope lives.

WHAT IS AN ENCYCLICAL?

An encyclical (pronounced: in-sik-li-cul) is a letter written by the Pope, often directed to the bishops, but intended for the whole Church and sometimes for all people.

WHO ARE THE MEN IN THE CHURCH WHO CONTINUE THE MISSION OF THE APOSTLES?

The men in the Church who continue the mission of the apostles are the Pope, who is the chief bishop, and all the other bishops united with him. They lead us in Jesus' name.

WHAT POWERS DO BISHOPS HAVE?

Bishops have all the powers of priests plus the power to ordain and to confirm.

WHAT DO BISHOPS DO?

Bishops lead and teach the Catholics of their dioceses. They encourage all Catholics to know and live their Faith. After the Pope, the bishops are the most important teachers in the Church. They are for us what the apostles were for the first Christians.

WHY ARE THE BISHOPS CALLED THE SUCCESSORS OF THE APOSTLES?

The bishops are called the successors of the apostles because they have received the apostles' positions. (A successor is a person who receives someone else's position.) (See: 1 Pt. 5:2-3.)

WHO ARE THE HIERARCHY?

The hierarchy are the Church's authorities—especially the Pope and bishops, but also priests and deacons.

WHAT IS MEANT BY THE MAGISTERIUM?

Magisterium refers to the teaching authority of the Church as vested in Christ's Vicar, the Pope, and the bishops, as successors of the Apostles, in union with the Holy Father.

WHAT IS MEANT BY THE "COLLEGE OF BISHOPS"?

By the "college of bishops" is meant that all of the bishops throughout the world united with the Pope form one body called the hierarchy or apostolic college.

WHAT IS THE "COLLEGE OF CARDINALS"?

"College of Cardinals" is the term used to mean all of the Cardinals as a united body. This body—chosen individually from among bishops and priests by the Pope to be his advisors—also elects a new Pope.

WHAT IS AN ECUMENICAL COUNCIL?

An ecumenical council is a meeting of the bishops of the whole world, called together by the Pope to discuss and explain Church teaching and to set forth guidelines for the People of God. An ecumenical council's conclusions have value only if approved by the Pope.

WHO IS A CARDINAL?

A Cardinal is a bishop (or priest) whom the Pope has chosen to belong to a special group of his advisors (and to elect a new Pope when the time comes).

WHO IS AN ARCHBISHOP?

An archbishop is usually the bishop of an important diocese (archdiocese), who has a certain amount of authority over the bishops of neighboring dioceses.

WHAT IS A DIOCESE OR ARCHDIOCESE?

A diocese or archdiocese is a territory made up of parishes placed by the Pope under the care of a Church leader called a bishop or archbishop.

WHAT IS A PARISH?

A parish is a community of Christians who worship together in the same Church and are led by the same priest, usually called a pastor. A diocesan priest serves the People of God in a parish.

WHO IS THE PASTOR?

The pastor is the chief priest or "shepherd" of a parish.

WHO IS THE VICAR GENERAL?

The Vicar General is an auxiliary bishop or priest appointed by a Cardinal or bishop to help him in the government of his diocese. For this reason, the Vicar General shares in the bishop's jurisdiction.

WHAT IS A CHANCERY OFFICE OF A DIOCESE OR ARCHDIOCESE?

A chancery office is the headquarters of the official business of a diocese or archdiocese in which Church transactions are recorded and carried out.

WHAT IS CANON LAW?

Canon Law is Church law found in the Code of Canon Law.

WHAT DOES THE WORD *IMPRIMATUR* MEAN?

Imprimatur means the permission of a bishop to print books regarding the Faith.

WHO IS A CATHOLIC?

A Catholic is a member of the Roman Catholic Church, which is distinguished from all other Christian churches by its loyalty to the Pope, who is the head of Jesus' Church because he is the successor of St. Peter. The earnest Catholic accepts what the Church teaches as coming from Christ Himself, and strives to conform his or her life to those teachings.

WHO ARE THE PEOPLE OF GOD?

The People of God, the "chosen people" of the New Covenant, are the members of the Church.

IS THE CATHOLIC CHURCH NECESSARY FOR SALVATION?

Yes, the Catholic Church is necessary for salvation, because all the grace that comes from Christ is communicated through His Church.

CAN PEOPLE BE SAVED WHO DO NOT BELONG TO THE CATHOLIC CHURCH?

People can be saved if through no fault of their own they do not know our Savior Jesus Christ and His Church, but they do seek God sincerely and try to live good lives with His help.

WHO ARE THE LAITY?

The laity are, in the ordinary sense of the word, all the Church's members who are not priests or religious.

WHO ARE THE EASTERN RITE CATHOLICS?

The Eastern Rite Catholics are groups united to the Pope who have the same beliefs as Western (Latin Rite) Catholics but differ slightly in the way they celebrate Mass and the sacraments as well as in various Church laws and customs.

WHO ARE THE EASTERN ORTHODOX CHRISTIANS?

The Eastern Orthodox Christians are non-Catholic Christians who separated from the Catholic Church in the Middle Ages. They have the Mass and the seven sacraments but do not accept the Pope as their chief leader.

WHAT IS ECUMENISM?

Ecumenism is the effort of Christians to become one united Church. It is also called the ecumenical movement.

WHAT DO WE MEAN WHEN WE SAY THAT A PERSON IS EXCOMMUNICATED?

When we say that a person is excommunicated, we mean that for some grave reason he or she may not receive the sacraments, especially the Holy Eucharist.

WHAT IS SCHISM?

A schism is a breaking away from the authority of the Pope and the unity (oneness) of the Church.

WHAT IS THE COMMUNION OF SAINTS?

The communion of saints is the communication of spiritual help among the members of Christ's body (the Church) in heaven, on earth and in purgatory.

WHAT IS A MARTYR?

A martyr is a person who allows himself or herself to be put to death rather than to deny the Christian Faith.

WHAT IS A MISSIONARY?

A missionary is a person dedicated to spreading God's Word (evangelizing), especially in the missions.

WHAT IS A MISSION?

A mission is an individual's purpose in life, which for Christ and the Christian is the saving of the world. A mission may also be a Christian community established to give non-Christian peoples the opportunity to learn about Jesus and salvation.

WHAT IS A SAINT?

A saint is a holy person on earth or in heaven, especially someone who grew so close to God on earth that the Church declared him or her a saint after death.

WHAT IS A PATRON SAINT?

A patron saint is a special person to imitate and pray to for help; a heavenly protector, usually one's name saint.

DEATH—AND THEN WHAT?

WHAT IS DEATH?

Death is the separation of soul and body, when the body of a human being becomes lifeless while the soul continues to live. The Bible says of God:

> You can turn man back into dust
> by saying, "Back to what you were, you sons of men!"
> (Ps. 90:3)**

WHAT IS A FUNERAL?

A funeral is the Mass for the deceased and the ceremonies connected with the burial of the dead.

WHAT IS A CEMETERY?

A cemetery is a place for burying the dead. For Catholics the ground or plot of land is to be consecrated or blessed.

WHAT IS CREMATION?

Cremation is the burning of a body, not encouraged by the Church except for good reasons.

WHAT IS THE FALSE BELIEF CALLED "REINCARNATION"?

The false belief called "reincarnation" is built upon the erroneous concept that the souls of the dead return to earth in new forms or bodies. It is also called "transmigration of souls."

WHAT AWAITS A PERSON AFTER DEATH AND INDIVIDUAL JUDGMENT?

After death and individual judgment, a person may go to heaven for all eternity; he may go to purgatory temporarily and then to heaven; or he may go to hell for all eternity.

WHAT IS THE PARTICULAR JUDGMENT?

The particular judgment is the judgment of a person by Christ immediately after death. It is also called the individual judgment.

...Men only die once, and after that comes judgment... (Heb. 9:27).**

WHAT IS THE GENERAL JUDGMENT?

The general or universal judgment is the event at the end of the world when God will make known everyone's eternal destiny in the presence of all mankind.

WILL OUR RESURRECTED BODIES BE THE SAME THEN AS THEY ARE NOW?

Our resurrected bodies will be ours, but transformed. The bodies of the just will be in a glorified state, which means that they will no longer have physical needs and will be endowed with qualities that they did not possess in their mortal existence.

...The dead will be raised incorruptible, and we shall be changed. This corruptible body must be clothed with incorruptibility, this mortal body with immortality (1 Cor. 15:52-53).*

WHAT IS MEANT BY THE "GLORIFIED BODY"?

The glorified body is the body of one who has risen from death to eternal life as have Jesus and Mary—as will the saints on the last day. The qualities of a glorified body will be:

impassibility: that is, freedom from suffering and death;

brightness: our body will shine like the sun, just as the body of Jesus shone at the Transfiguration;

agility: our bodies will be able to go from one place to another with the speed of thought;

and *subtilty:* being so spiritualized that they will be able to pass through matter without dividing it, just as Jesus entered the Cenacle through locked doors. The glory of each will be determined by the holiness achieved during life.

HAS THE BODY OF ANY HUMAN PERSON BEEN PRESERVED FROM CORRUPTION AND TAKEN INTO HEAVEN?

By a very special privilege, the body of one human person has been preserved from corruption and taken into heaven. That person is the Blessed Virgin Mary. This special privilege—proclaimed a dogma of faith by Pope Pius XII on November 1, 1950—is called her Assumption. This feast is celebrated every year on August 15.

WHAT IS A DOGMA OF FAITH?

A dogma of Faith is a doctrine formally stated and authoritatively proclaimed to all Catholics by the Church.

WHAT WILL HAPPEN AT THE END OF THE WORLD?

At the end of the world the bodies of all people will rise from the earth to be reunited to their souls forever. The bodies of the just will share in the souls' glory; the bodies of the damned will share the punishment.

"...An hour is coming
in which all those in their tombs
shall hear his voice and come forth.
Those who have done right shall rise to live;
the evildoers shall rise to be damned" (Jn. 5:28-29).*

WHAT WILL FOLLOW THE LAST JUDGMENT?

After the last judgment there will be only heaven and hell. The just will share the bliss of heaven forever; the damned will share everlasting suffering.

WHEN WILL THE END OF THE WORLD OCCUR?

When the world will end is not known to us.

"...As for that day and hour, nobody knows it..." (Mt. 24:36).**

WHAT IS MEANT BY "ETERNAL"?

"Eternal" means without beginning or end.

WHAT IS MEANT BY ETERNITY?

By eternity we mean no beginning, end or change. This is the way we use it when we are talking about God's eternity. It can also mean the condition of angels and men, who had a beginning but will always continue existing through God's power.

WHAT IS THE BEATIFIC VISION?

The Beatific Vision is the clear and immediate vision and experience of God enjoyed by the angels and saints in heaven.

WHO ARE THE "BLESSED"?

The "blessed" are the souls of the dead who are in heaven. It is also the title given to a person who has been beatified or declared "blessed" by the Church.

HOW LONG WILL HEAVEN AND HELL LAST?

Heaven and hell are everlasting.

ARE WE WHO ARE STILL ON EARTH ABLE TO HELP THE SOULS IN PURGATORY?

We on earth can help the souls in purgatory with our prayers, especially the offering of the Mass, and acts of charity for them.

ARE WE WHO ARE STILL ON EARTH ABLE TO HELP THE SOULS IN HELL?

We who are still on earth are not able to help the souls in hell. They cannot be helped.

WHAT IS LIMBO?

Limbo is the place where the souls of good people waited until Jesus' death-resurrection opened heaven to them; also a place where (some think) the souls of the unbaptized children enjoy a natural happiness much less perfect than the joys of heaven.

WHAT IS THE "PAIN OF LOSS"?

The "pain of loss" is one of the sufferings of those in hell or purgatory. It is awareness of being separated from our good and loving God.

WHAT IS THE "PAIN OF SENSE"?

The "pain of sense" is the term used to express the other sufferings of hell or purgatory, a torment that is, or feels like, physical pain.

WHAT IS HELL?

Hell is everlasting suffering and separation from God.

WHO ARE THE DAMNED?

The damned are those who suffer everlasting punishment in hell.

"Then he will say to those on his left: 'Out of my sight, you condemned, into that everlasting fire prepared for the devil and his angels!' " (Mt. 25:41)* (See also: 2 Thes. 1:6-10.)

WHY SHOULD WE WANT TO GO TO HEAVEN?

We should want to go to heaven because in heaven we will be totally fulfilled in God; we will be perfectly happy praising Him forever. St. Paul says:

Now we are seeing a dim reflection in a mirror; but then we shall be seeing face to face (1 Cor. 13:12).**

IS THERE ANY PAIN, SORROW OR SIN IN HEAVEN?

In heaven there is no pain, sorrow, sin or whatever could cause unhappiness. There cannot even be the threat cr fear of these things.

WILL WE KNOW OUR FAMILY AND FRIENDS IN HEAVEN?

We will know our family and friends in heaven, and we will rejoice with them in God.

COULD LIFE IN HEAVEN BE BORING?

Life in heaven could never be boring because we will always be finding out new and wonderful things about God.

WHOSE COMPANY WILL THE "BLESSED" IN HEAVEN ENJOY?

The "blessed" in heaven will enjoy the company of Jesus, their Savior, and His Mother, as well as all the angels, saints, His relatives and friends.

WILL EVERYONE HAVE THE SAME DEGREE OF HAPPINESS IN HEAVEN?

Everyone will not have the same degree or amount of happiness in heaven, but all will be perfectly happy.

WHO WILL HAVE GREATER HAPPINESS IN HEAVEN?
They will have greater happiness in heaven who loved God more unselfishly on earth.

WHAT IS PURGATORY?
Purgatory is a condition of suffering after death in which souls make up for their sins before they enter heaven.

WHO GO TO PURGATORY?
They go to purgatory who have unrepented venial sins or who have not as yet sufficiently paid for the temporal punishment due to their sins.

HOW LONG WILL PURGATORY LAST?
Purgatory will last until the general judgment. Each soul in purgatory stays there only until his debt of justice to God is paid.

The Sacraments

THE SACRAMENTS—ACTIONS OF JESUS

HOW CAN WE GROW IN GRACE, VIRTUE AND THE SEVEN GIFTS OF THE HOLY SPIRIT?

We can grow in grace, virtue and the seven gifts of the Holy Spirit by receiving the sacraments, praying and doing good deeds.

WHAT ARE THE SACRAMENTS?

The sacraments are sacred signs through which Jesus gives us His Spirit and makes us holy and pleasing to Him by grace.

WHAT IS A SACRAMENTAL "SIGN"?

A sacramental *sign* is something that we can hear or see, etc., and which tells us something about the sacrament we are about to receive. In every sacrament words make up part of the sign.

WHAT DOES "HOLY" MEAN?

Holy means "like God" or "close to God." It can also mean "set apart." God's holiness is the greatness and goodness that sets Him apart from all His creatures.

Through the sacraments Jesus makes His people *holy* by grace. Through some of the sacraments Jesus also forgives sins, and through all of them He gives help to avoid sin.

CAN WE BE SURE OF RECEIVING GRACE THROUGH THE SACRAMENTS?

Jesus always gives grace through the sacraments if we receive them under the proper conditions (such as freedom from mortal sin for the receiving of Communion, and other conditions). How greatly the sacrament and its grace will affect us depends on our own *attitude* — for example, how much faith and love we have.

HOW MANY SACRAMENTS ARE THERE?

There are seven sacraments.

WHAT ARE THE NAMES OF THE SEVEN SACRAMENTS?

The seven sacraments are: Baptism, Confirmation, Holy Eucharist, Penance, Anointing of the Sick, Holy Orders and Matrimony.

WHO GAVE US THE SACRAMENTS?

Jesus gave us the sacraments and continues to give each one of them. He does this through the Church.

With regard to some of the sacraments, we know from Scripture that Jesus instituted them. Tradition tells us that He instituted them *all.*

MAY THE SACRAMENTS BE DIVIDED INTO GROUPS?

The sacraments may be divided into three groups. Baptism, Confirmation and Eucharist are sacraments of *initiation,* or beginning in the Christian life.

Penance and the Anointing of the Sick are sacraments of *reconciliation,* or peace-making.

Holy Orders and Matrimony are sacraments of *vocation,* or calling to a particular way of life.

MAY WE ALSO SPEAK OF THE CHURCH AS A "SACRAMENT"?

We may also speak of the Church as a "sacrament" — a "great sacrament" through which we receive the other seven. The Church is a sign that there is a God, and that He cares about the world. The sacraments, too, are signs of God's loving concern for people.

BAPTISM

WHAT IS BAPTISM?

Baptism is the sacrament in which Jesus sends us His Spirit, who frees us from sin and gives us the grace by which we become God's children, heirs of heaven, members of the Church and temples of the Blessed Trinity.

FROM WHAT SINS DOES JESUS SET US FREE IN BAPTISM?

In Baptism Jesus sets us free from original sin and all personal sins we have committed before being baptized.

Blessed be God the Father of our Lord Jesus Christ, who in his great mercy has given us a new birth as his sons... (1 Pt. 1:3).**

WHAT DO WE RECEIVE AT BAPTISM?

At Baptism we receive sanctifying grace, the theological or God-given virtues, and the seven gifts of the Holy Spirit.

In Baptism we also receive a lasting *spiritual seal,* called a *character,* which sets us apart as belonging to Jesus Christ. This is the character, or seal, of a *Christian.* (A Christian is a follower of Jesus Christ.)

See what love the Father has bestowed on us
in letting us be called children of God!
Yet that is what we are (1 Jn. 3:1).*

WHAT MAKES UP THE SIGN OF BAPTISM?

The sign of Baptism is made up of water and words.

WHAT DO THE WATER AND WORDS STAND FOR?

The water stands for the removal of sin and the giving of new life called *grace.* The words show that the person is entering into a new and lasting relationship with our triune God—Father, Son and Holy Spirit.

IS BAPTISM NECESSARY?

Baptism is necessary because it takes away original sin which every person inherits from Adam and Eve. Original sin must be taken away before we get to heaven.

In addition we are given the life of grace, made children of God, and incorporated into Christ and His Church.

"...You must be baptized in the name of Jesus Christ for the forgiveness of your sins..." (Acts 2:38).**

SINCE BAPTISM IS NECESSARY TO GET TO HEAVEN, WHAT WILL HAPPEN TO THOSE PEOPLE WHO, THROUGH NO FAULT OF THEIR OWN, HAVE NOT RECEIVED IT? CAN THEY BE SAVED?

Those who through no fault of their own have not received the sacrament of Baptism can be saved through what is called Baptism of Blood or Baptism of Desire.

WHAT IS BAPTISM OF BLOOD?

Baptism of Blood is the reception of grace by an unbaptized person because he or she gives his or her life for love of Christ or a Christian virtue.

WHAT IS BAPTISM OF DESIRE?

Baptism of Desire is the reception of grace because of perfect love of God and the desire to do His will. In other words, if the person knew of Baptism and were able to receive it, he would be baptized.

WHY DOES THE CHURCH BAPTIZE INFANTS?

The Church baptizes infants in order that they may be reborn to the divine life of grace in Christ Jesus and become heirs of heaven.

IS THERE A DANGER IN PUTTING OFF THE BAPTISM OF INFANTS FOR A LONG PERIOD OF TIME?

Children should be baptized as soon as reasonably possible after birth. Catholic parents who put off for a long time, or entirely neglect, the Baptism of their children may put them in the danger of losing the vision of God eternally.

HOW IS BAPTISM GIVEN?

Baptism is given by pouring water on the forehead, while saying the necessary words: "I baptize you in the name of the Father, and of the Son, and of the Holy Spirit." (It also may be given by sprinkling the forehead, or by dipping the crown of the head.)

When Baptism is given in Church, there are many parts to the beautiful ceremony. But the necessary part is the saying of the words at the same time that the water flows on the forehead.

SHOULD AN INFANT BE BAPTIZED WITHOUT THE PERMISSION OF A PARENT OR GUARDIAN?

An infant should not be baptized without the permission of a parent or guardian, except when in danger of death. It is the parent or guardian who must see to the Christian upbringing of a baptized child.

WHAT HAPPENS TO INFANTS WHO DIE UNBAPTIZED?

Since infants who die unbaptized have committed no sins, many have held that they will live in a place of natural happiness called "Limbo." Some modern scholars suggest that God will grant these infants the possibility of heaven by Baptism of Desire before death. The Church has made no official declaration on the matter.

WHO MAY RECEIVE BAPTISM?

Any unbaptized person may receive Baptism. If this person has reached what is called the "age of reason"—able to understand—he or she must also *want* to receive the sacrament and have faith and sorrow for sin with the intention of avoiding future sin.

CAN WE BE BAPTIZED MORE THAN ONCE?

We cannot be baptized more than once, due to the indelible spiritual seal we received at Baptism.

WHO MAY ADMINISTER THE SACRAMENT OF BAPTISM?

The bishop, priest or deacon is the usual minister of Baptism, but in the danger of death anyone may and sometimes *should* baptize. No one, however, may baptize himself.

IN AN EMERGENCY, DOES THE PERSON WHO BAPTIZES HAVE TO BE A CATHOLIC?

In an emergency, the person who baptizes can be anyone—man, woman or child, Catholic or non-Catholic, atheist or pagan—as long as he or she administers the sacrament properly and does it with the intention of "doing what the Church does."

HOW IS EMERGENCY BAPTISM GIVEN?

Emergency Baptism is given by pouring ordinary water three times on the forehead of the person to be baptized, saying while pouring it: "I baptize you in the name of the Father, and of the Son, and of the Holy Spirit." The words must be said at the same time the water is poured.

IS BAPTISM THAT IS ADMINISTERED BY A LAY PERSON AS VALID AS THAT ADMINISTERED BY THE PRIEST?

Yes. When properly given, Baptism administered by a lay person is as valid as Baptism given by a priest.

WHAT IS CONDITIONAL BAPTISM?

Conditional Baptism is the giving of Baptism on the condition that it can be received (using such words as: "If you are not baptized, I baptize you..." or "If you are alive, I baptize you...").

WHO ARE CATECHUMENS?

Catechumens are unbaptized persons who are taking instructions to become Catholics.

WHAT DO WE MEAN BY THE BAPTISMAL CHARACTER?

The baptismal character is a lasting spiritual seal, which marks a person as a Christian for life. Other sacraments which impose a lasting seal are Confirmation and Holy Orders.

WHAT IS THE BAPTISMAL ROBE?

The baptismal robe is the white garment given to the newly-baptized as a symbol of grace and innocence.

WHAT IS BAPTISMAL WATER?

Baptismal water is blessed for use in Baptism, but in case of emergency, any water may be used.

WHAT IS A BAPTISTRY?

A baptistry is the part of the Church (or separate building) in which Baptism takes place.

WHAT IS CHRISM?

Chrism is a blessed mixture of oil and balm used during the baptismal ceremony, in Confirmation, during the ordination of bishops, and in the consecration of churches, altars, etc.

WHAT ARE THE BAPTISMAL PROMISES?

The baptismal promises are promises to renounce the devil, his allurements or temptations, and to live according to the teachings of Christ and His Church.

DO CONVERTS HAVE TO BE BAPTIZED AGAIN?

Christian converts to the Catholic Faith do not have to be baptized again if their first Baptism was valid, that is, given with the use of water (made to flow on the skin), together with the form of Baptism, performed with the intention of doing what the Church does.

WHAT IS A GODPARENT?

A godparent serves as a representative of the community of faith. At an ordinary Baptism there must be at least one.

WHAT ARE THE DUTIES OF GODPARENTS?

Godparents have the duty of making sure that the child is given a good Catholic upbringing if the parents die or fail in their Christian duty toward the child. Godparents should themselves be good Catholics.

CAN AN ADULT BE ADMITTED TO BAPTISM WITHOUT A GODPARENT?

An adult should not be admitted to Baptism without a godparent. This is a very ancient custom in the Catholic Church. The godparent helps the person prepare well for Baptism and afterward aids him to persevere in the faith and in his life as a Christian.

WHAT DOES THE CHURCH REQUIRE IN ORDER TO BE A GODPARENT?

In order to be a godparent, the Church requires that the person be mature enough to take on the responsibility; that he or she be a member of the Catholic Church, and have already received Baptism, Confirmation and Eucharist.

MAY A NON-CATHOLIC ACT AS A GODPARENT?

If the non-Catholic is a baptized and believing Christian from a separated Church he (she) may act as a Christian witness, if this is requested by the parents, along with a Catholic godparent. (The norms for various ecumenical cases should be followed.)

WHAT DOES A GODPARENT DO AT THE BAPTISM?

A godparent testifies to the faith of the one to be baptized, or in the case of an infant he, together with the child's parents, professes the faith of the Church.

WHAT DO WE MEAN BY THE EXPRESSION "CHRISTIAN NAME"?

By the expression "Christian name" we mean the name received at Baptism.

WHY IS A SAINT'S NAME GIVEN IN BAPTISM?

A saint's name is given in Baptism so that the new Christian will have a protector in heaven to imitate and ask for help.

WHAT DOES THE WORD "CHRISTENING" MEAN?

Christening is another name for Baptism.

WHAT VIRTUES DO WE RECEIVE AT BAPTISM?

At Baptism we receive the theological virtues and cardinal virtues.

THE EUCHARIST

HOW IS JESUS STILL WITH US?

Jesus is still with us in His Church, in His Word, in the seven sacraments, in the Christian community, in the needy, and in other ways, but most especially in the Holy Eucharist.

WHAT IS THE HOLY EUCHARIST?

The Holy Eucharist is a sacrament, a sacrifice, and the abiding presence of Jesus Himself, God and man. He is truly and completely present under the appearances of bread and wine, to make us more like Himself and to join us to one another.

Jesus said:
"I am the bread of life.
He who comes to me will never be hungry;
he who believes in me will never thirst" (Jn. 6:35).**

WHY DID JESUS GIVE US THE HOLY EUCHARIST?

Jesus gave us the Holy Eucharist because He wanted to stay close to His followers until the end of time to teach us, comfort us, strengthen us and make us holy.

He said:
"I am the bread of life.
He who comes to me will never be hungry;
he who believes in me will never thirst" (Jn. 6:35).**

HOW IS THE EUCHARIST DIFFERENT FROM ALL THE OTHER SACRAMENTS?

The Eucharist is different from all the other sacraments because under the appearances of bread and wine Jesus is completely present as both God and man. In the other sacraments, He is present only by His power and its effects. Jesus said:

"I am the bread of life...

the living bread which has come down from heaven. Anyone who eats this bread will live for ever"

(Jn. 6:35, 51).**

IS THE EUCHARIST IMPORTANT?

The Eucharist "is of the greatest importance for the uniting and strengthening of the Church" (Basic Teachings, n. 12).

WHAT IS CORPUS CHRISTI?

Corpus Christi is Latin for the Body of Christ. It is also a day dedicated by the Church for giving praise and thanks to the Holy Eucharist in a special way; it is celebrated on the second Sunday after Pentecost (in the United States).

WHAT DO THE WORDS OF CONSECRATION TELL US?

The words of Consecration—"This is my body which will be given up for you"...; "This is the cup of my blood.... It will be shed for you..."—tell us that the Eucharist is the body and blood of Jesus, and that Christ is offered in sacrifice.

WHAT IS TRANSUBSTANTIATION?

Transubstantiation is the changing of the entire substance of bread and wine into Christ's body and blood. This takes place at Mass at the words of Consecration.

WHAT IS THE MASS OR EUCHARISTIC CELEBRATION?

The Mass or Eucharistic Celebration is:

— the sacrifice of the cross taking place today on our altars;

— a memorial of Jesus' death, resurrection and ascension;

— a holy covenant meal or banquet in which we receive Jesus Himself.

WHAT ARE SOME OTHER NAMES FOR THE MASS?

Other names for the Mass include: "the Liturgy," "Eucharistic Celebration," and "Eucharistic Sacrifice." Liturgy means "service."

WHAT DOES THE WORD "EUCHARIST" MEAN?

The word *Eucharist,* which we use for Christ fully present under the appearances of bread and wine, means "thanksgiving."

WHEN WAS THE FIRST MASS CELEBRATED?

The first Mass was celebrated by Jesus Himself at the Last Supper on Holy Thursday evening, the night before He died.

Then he took some bread, and when he had given thanks, broke it and gave it to them, saying, "This is my body which will be given for you; do this as a memorial of me." He did the same with the cup after supper, and said, "This cup is the new covenant in my blood which will be poured out for you" (Lk. 22:19-20).**

WHO WERE PRESENT AT THE FIRST EUCHARISTIC CELEBRATION?

The apostles were present at the first Eucharistic Celebration.

When the hour came he took his place at table, and the apostles with him (Lk. 22:14).** (See also: Mk. 14:17).

WHY DOES CHRIST RENEW HIS SACRIFICE TO-DAY?

Christ renews His sacrifice for us and for our world, so that, in the best way possible, that is, through Him, with Him, and in Him, we can adore and thank the Father, ask His forgiveness and ask His help. St. Paul wrote:

For this is what I received from the Lord, and in turn passed on to you: that on the same night that he was betrayed, the Lord Jesus took some bread, and thanked God for it and broke it, and he said, "This is my body, which is for you; do this as a memorial of me." In the same way he took the cup after supper, and said, "This cup is the new covenant in my blood. Whenever you drink it, do this as a memorial of me" (1 Cor. 11:23-25).**

HOW DOES CHRIST RENEW THE SACRIFICE OF THE CROSS?

Christ renews the sacrifice of the cross in the Mass in an unbloody manner for our sake.

...He forever lives to make intercession for them (Heb. 7:25).*

WHAT IS MEANT BY THE SACRIFICE OF CALVARY?

By the sacrifice of Calvary we mean Jesus' death on the cross, for our sins, which is renewed in every Eucharistic Celebration.

...Christ...offered himself as the perfect sacrifice to God... (Heb. 9:14).**

WHY IS JESUS CALLED THE LAMB OF GOD AT EVERY EUCHARISTIC CELEBRATION?

Jesus is called the Lamb of God, because He was slain like the Old Testament Passover Lamb, and His Paschal Mystery saved us from the slavery of sin. St. Paul said:

Christ our Passover has been sacrificed (1 Cor. 5:7).* (See also: Is. 53:7, Jn. 1:36, Rv. 5:12.)

WHAT ARE THE MAIN PURPOSES OF THE MASS?

The main purposes of the Mass are:

— to adore (praise) God

— to thank Him

— to ask His forgiveness and atone (make up) for sin

— to ask His help for ourselves and others.

WHY IS JESUS PRESENT AT MASS UNDER THE APPEARANCES OF ORDINARY FOOD AND DRINK?

Jesus is present at Mass under the appearances of ordinary food and drink to encourage us to receive Him as the spiritual food necessary for a truly Christian life. That is why

...anyone who eats the bread or drinks the cup of the Lord unworthily will be behaving unworthily towards the body and blood of the Lord (1 Cor. 11:27).**

WHY DOES THE MASS OR EUCHARISTIC SACRIFICE CONTINUE TO BE CELEBRATED?

The Mass or Eucharistic Sacrifice "is carried out in obedience to the words of Jesus at the Last Supper: 'Do this in memory of me' " (Basic Teachings, no. 12).

WHO IS THE CELEBRANT OF THE MASS?

The celebrant is another name for the priest who is offering or "celebrating" the Eucharistic Sacrifice.

WHAT ARE THE PRESIDENTIAL PRAYERS OF THE MASS?

The presidential prayers are the prayers of the Eucharistic Celebration which can be said only by a priest, for example, the Eucharistic Prayer.

WHAT ARE THE FRUITS OF OUR PARTICIPATING IN THE MASS WITH ATTENTION AND LOVE?

Participating in the Mass with attention and love can help us:

— to avoid temptations and sin

— to find peace of mind and heart

— to grow in the love of God

— to obtain protection against all dangers

— to gain the help we need from God

— to shorten the Purgatory of departed family members and friends.

WHY IS THE MASS SO POWERFUL?

The Mass is so powerful because in it Jesus Himself prays to the Father for us.

BECAUSE OF THE IMPORTANCE OF THE MASS, WHAT DOES THE CHURCH OBLIGE OF US?

Because of the importance of the Mass, the Church obliges us to go to Mass on Sundays and holy days of obligation. (For a listing of the holy days in the United States, see page 21.)

SHOULD A CATHOLIC, FOR ANY REASON, STOP GOING TO MASS?

No Catholic, for any reason, should stop going to Mass. Even persons who cannot receive the sacraments (for example, because of divorce and remarriage) should assist at Mass to ask God's mercy and help.

PARTS OF THE MASS

WHAT IS MEANT BY THE INTRODUCTORY RITE OF THE MASS?

By the Introductory Rite of the Mass we mean the part of the Eucharistic Celebration which includes Entrance Song, Greeting of the People, Penitential Rite or Rite of Blessing and Sprinkling Holy Water, "Lord, Have Mercy," "Glory to God" and Opening Prayer. The Introductory Rite prepares the faith-community to hear God's Word and to participate at the Eucharist.

WHAT IS MEANT BY THE PENITENTIAL RITE OF THE MASS?

The Penitential Rite of the Mass is that part of the Introductory Rite in which we call to mind our sins and ask God to have mercy on us. This Rite can take away venial sin, but not serious (mortal) sin. Each serious sin must be confessed in the sacrament of Penance or Confession.

WHAT IS THE RITE OF BLESSING AND SPRINKLING HOLY WATER AT MASS?

The Rite of Blessing and Sprinkling Holy Water may be used at Mass instead of the Penitential Rite. It reminds us of our Baptism.

WHAT IS THE LITURGY OF THE WORD?

The Liturgy of the Word is that part of the Mass which includes readings from Scripture, Responsorial Psalm, Alleluia or Gospel Acclamation, Homily, Profession of Faith and General Intercessions or Prayer of the Faithful.

WHAT IS THE RESPONSORIAL PSALM?

The Responsorial Psalm is a psalm from Scripture said by the worshipping community after the first reading, during the Liturgy of the Word.

WHAT IS THE HOMILY?

The *homily* is that part of the Mass in which the priest explains the Word of God just proclaimed.

WHAT IS THE PROFESSION OF FAITH PROCLAIMED AT THE MASS?

The Profession of Faith or Creed is said by the faithful to express belief in the truths of our Catholic Faith and in the word of God just proclaimed in the readings.

WHAT IS THE PRAYER OF THE FAITHFUL OR GENERAL INTERCESSIONS?

The Prayer of the Faithful or General Intercessions is a special prayer by which the faithful act as a priestly people and intercede, or ask God's help, for all the needs of the Church and the world.

WHAT IS THE LITURGY OF THE EUCHARIST?

The Liturgy of the Eucharist is the very important part of the Mass that follows the Liturgy of the Word. Within the Eucharistic Prayer, our gifts of bread and wine become the body and blood of Jesus, offered in sacrifice to God. At Communion, we receive Jesus as a sign of our unity with Christ and with one another.

WHAT DO WE MEAN BY THE PREPARATION OF THE ALTAR AND GIFTS?

The Preparation of the Altar and Gifts is that part of the Mass in which the gifts of bread and wine are carried to the altar, the altar is prepared, and the priest washes his hands and prays to be cleansed of sin.

WHAT IS THE PREFACE OF THE MASS?

The Preface of the Mass is a prayer of praise and thanks to God our Father for the work of salvation or for some particular aspect of His saving love; it is also part of the Eucharistic Prayer.

WHAT IS THE PREFACE ACCLAMATION?

The Preface Acclamation or "Holy, Holy, Holy" is a wonderful song in which priest and people join their praise of God to that of the angels.

WHAT IS THE EUCHARISTIC PRAYER?

The Eucharistic Prayer is a hymn of thanksgiving to God for His work of salvation. Within this great prayer, bread and wine are changed into the Body and Blood of Christ.

WHAT IS THE CONSECRATION OF THE MASS?

The Consecration is that sacred part of the Eucharistic Sacrifice in which the words of the priest: "This is my Body"; "this is my Blood" change bread and wine into the Body and Blood of Christ.

WHAT IS MEANT BY THE MEMORIAL ACCLAMATION?

The Memorial Acclamation is that part of the Eucharistic Prayer in which the priest invites: "Let us proclaim the mystery of faith," and we respond: "Christ has died, Christ is risen, Christ will come again," or a similar acclamation.

WHAT IS THE FINAL DOXOLOGY?

The final doxology is a tribute of praise to our triune God proclaimed through, with and in Christ. This concludes the Eucharistic Prayer; the Communion Rite follows.

WHAT IS THE COMMUNION RITE?

The Communion Rite is that part of the Liturgy of the Eucharist which includes the Lord's Prayer, the Rite of Peace, Breaking of the Bread, the Lamb of God, the Communion of the priest and people, and the Prayer after Communion.

WHAT IS THE RITE OF PEACE?

The Rite of Peace is an expression of love and peace which members of the community give each other at Mass before sharing the body and blood of Jesus.

WHAT IS THAT PART OF THE MASS CALLED THE BREAKING OF THE BREAD?

The Breaking of the Bread is that part of the Communion Rite of the Mass in which the priest breaks the sacred bread as a sign that in Communion we become one in the body and blood of Christ.

WHAT IS HOLY COMMUNION?

Holy Communion is the real Eucharistic Jesus whom we receive at Mass.

WHAT IS THE CONCLUDING RITE OF THE MASS?

The Concluding Rite of the Mass is the priest's blessing and dismissal of the people, inviting them to do good works and to praise God.

RECEIVING THE EUCHARIST

WHY DOES JESUS COME TO US IN THE EUCHARIST?

Jesus comes to us in the Eucharist to give us new spiritual energy so that we can continue leading good Christian lives.

DO WE NEED THE HELP OF THE EUCHARIST?

We do need the help of the Eucharist very much. Temptations and difficulties can "wear us down" in spirit. Communion helps us to go ahead with new strength and courage. Receiving the Eucharist, we also grow in love for all God's people. The Eucharist joins the whole Church more closely together. Jesus said:

"I tell you most solemnly,
if you do not eat the flesh of the Son of Man
and drink his blood,
you will not have life in you.
This is the bread come down from heaven;...
anyone who eats this bread will live for ever"
(Jn. 6:53, 58).**

WHAT MUST WE DO TO RECEIVE THE HOLY EUCHARIST WORTHILY?

To receive the Holy Eucharist worthily we must:

— Believe that Jesus is really present in the Holy Eucharist

— Be free from serious sin

— Fast before receiving Holy Communion, out of respect for the Son of God, the Second Person of the Blessed Trinity, who comes to us in Holy Communion. This means not to eat or drink anything except water for one hour before receiving Communion. Water may be taken at any time. (This regulation is not for people who are old or ill and cannot fast.)

HOW SHOULD A PERSON RECEIVE THE EUCHARIST?

A person should receive the Eucharist with faith, reverence and love.

We show our faith by answering "Amen" after the priest, deacon or lay minister has said, "The body of Christ." We show our reverence by the respectful way we receive Communion.

We show our love by talking silently with Jesus after we have received Him, and by carrying His love into our daily actions.

WHAT ARE THE RIGHTS AND PRIVILEGES OF CATHOLICS WHO HAVE MADE THEIR FIRST COMMUNION?

Catholics who have made their first Communion have become active members of the worshipping community. They may receive Communion often—even every day—provided they are in the state of grace.

WHAT ARE THE DUTIES AND RESPONSIBILITIES OF CATHOLICS WHO HAVE MADE THEIR FIRST COMMUNION?

Catholics who have made their first Communion are to take part in the Mass every Sunday (or Saturday night) and receive Communion at least once a year (in Lent or the Easter Season).

HOW OFTEN SHOULD WE RECEIVE JESUS IN HOLY COMMUNION?

We should receive Jesus in Holy Communion often, even every day, because it is Jesus who makes us holy by giving us His life and grace. Jesus said:

"I came
that they might have life
and have it to the full" (Jn. 10:10).*

WHAT IS MEANT BY EASTER DUTY?

By Easter duty is meant the duty of receiving Holy Communion at least once a year—between the first Sunday of Lent and the Sunday after Pentecost (Trinity Sunday).

WHAT IS VIATICUM?

Viaticum is Communion given to a person in danger of death.

JESUS REMAINS IN THE TABERNACLE

DOES THE EUCHARIST REMAIN IN THE CHURCH AFTER MASS?

The Eucharist does remain in the church after Mass, in the tabernacle.

WHAT IS ANOTHER NAME FOR THE EUCHARIST?

Another name for the Eucharist is the Blessed Sacrament. The Blessed Sacrament is one of the great treasures of our Catholic Faith.

IS PRAYER BEFORE THE BLESSED SACRAMENT BENEFICIAL?

Prayer before the Blessed Sacrament brings great comfort and strength, because in the Eucharist Jesus is fully present. He is there to listen to us and help us.

WHAT IS THE TABERNACLE?

The tabernacle is the box-like shrine in which Jesus, in the Blessed Sacrament, is kept.

WHAT IS A MONSTRANCE?

A monstrance is a tall vessel in which the Blessed Sacrament may be placed for adoration (also called an Ostensorium—both words have the meaning of ''showing'').

HOW SHOULD WE SHOW OUR LOVE AND THANK-FULNESS TO JESUS FOR REMAINING IN THE TABERNACLE?

We should show our love and thankfulness to Jesus for remaining in the tabernacle by making frequent visits to Church, by being respectful and prayerful, by participating often in the Eucharistic Celebration, and attending parish devotions.

WHAT IS EUCHARISTIC BENEDICTION?

Eucharistic Benediction is the ceremony in which the priest blesses the people with the consecrated host enclosed in a sacred vessel called a monstrance which is visible to the worshipping community.

WHAT IS A GENUFLECTION?

A genuflection is showing reverence by bending the right knee to the floor (especially done when passing in front of the Blessed Sacrament).

LITURGICAL VESSELS AND VESTMENTS USED AT MASS

WHAT ARE VESTMENTS?

Vestments are special robes worn to celebrate the Eucharist. Every priest celebrating Mass must wear the alb, stole and chasuble.

WHAT IS A STOLE?

A stole is a long, narrow band of the same material and color as the chasuble. It is worn around the priest's neck and crossed over his chest.

WHAT IS A CINCTURE?

The cincture is a long cord used to gather the alb at the priest's waist.

WHAT IS A CHASUBLE?

The chasuble is the outer vestment of the priest celebrating Mass.

WHAT IS AN AMICE?

An amice is a square piece of white cloth that is tucked into the priest's collar and covers his shoulders.

WHAT IS AN ALB?

The alb is a long white tunic or robe which the priest wears while offering the Eucharistic Sacrifice.

WHAT IS A DALMATIC?

A dalmatic is a vestment worn by the deacon over the alb and stole at liturgical celebrations.

WHAT IS AN ALTAR?

An altar is the table of the Lord, made of marble, granite, wood or another solid, attractive material. The People of God are called together to share in the offering of the Lord Jesus at this altar of sacrifice. Usually, relics of martyrs or saints are put inside the altar.

WHY IS THE CROSS WITH THE FIGURE OF THE BODY OF CHRIST PLACED ON THE ALTAR OR NEAR IT?

The cross with the figure of the Body of Christ is placed on the altar or near it, to remind the worshipping community of Jesus' Sacrifice of the Cross.

WHAT MEANING DO THE LIT CANDLES ON THE ALTAR HAVE?

The lighted candles witness to our devotion to Jesus who is light and life with His grace.

WHAT IS A LECTERN?

A lectern is a pulpit from which the Liturgy of the Word is proclaimed.

WHAT IS A LECTOR?

A lector is a lay person who proclaims God's Word (other than the Gospel) at Mass.

WHAT ARE THE CRUETS?

The cruets are small pitchers containing the wine and water used during the Eucharistic Celebration.

WHAT KIND OF BREAD MUST BE USED TO CELEBRATE THE EUCHARIST?

The bread used to celebrate the Eucharist must be made only of wheaten flour and water. Nothing else may be substituted or added.

WHAT KIND OF WINE MUST BE USED TO CELEBRATE THE EUCHARIST?

Pure, natural grape wine must be used to celebrate the Eucharist. Such wine, made for sacramental purposes, should be clearly designated as altar wine.

WHAT IS THE CHALICE?

The chalice is the sacred cup in which the wine becomes the true blood of Christ at the Consecration.

WHAT IS THE CIBORIUM?

The ciborium is a cup with a matching lid, used to hold the Body of Christ that will be given to the faith-community in Holy Communion.

WHAT IS THE CORPORAL?

The corporal is a piece of linen cloth on which the Body of Christ is placed.

WHAT IS A PALL?

A pall is a linen card about six inches square used to cover the chalice containing the precious Blood.

WHAT IS THE PATEN?

The paten is the dish upon which the Body of Jesus is placed.

WHAT IS A PURIFICATOR?

A purificator is a small linen towel that the priest uses to cleanse the sacred vessels.

WHAT IS A SANCTUARY LAMP?

A sanctuary lamp is a candle which continuously burns near the tabernacle where the Blessed Sacrament is kept.

WHAT IS MEANT BY LITURGICAL COLORS?

Liturgical colors, usually green, purple, red, rose and white, are colors of the priest's outer vestment which help to set the tone of joy, penance, etc., for particular liturgical seasons or feasts.

WHAT IS MEANT BY THE LITURGICAL YEAR?

The Liturgical Year is the name given to the days and seasons within a year's time in which the Church celebrates Christ's Paschal Mystery. The liturgical seasons are Advent, Christmas, Lent, Easter and Ordinary Time. Sundays and holydays, feasts of Mary, celebrations of saints' days and other feast days light the Church year with warmth to stir the devotion of God's people.

WHAT IS ADVENT?

"Advent" means *coming.* It is the season in which we prepare for Christmas.

WHAT IS CHRISTMAS?

Christmas is the holyday of obligation on which we celebrate Jesus' birth.

WHAT IS THE CHRISTMAS SEASON?

The Christmas Season is the joyful season from Christmas to the celebration of Jesus' baptism.

WHAT IS LENT?

Lent is the Church's season of preparation for Easter, in which Christians are expected to give more attention to prayer, penance and good deeds.

WHAT IS EASTER?

Easter, the Church's greatest day of celebration, is the special Sunday on which we rejoice over Jesus' resurrection from the dead.

WHAT IS THE EASTER SEASON?

The Easter Season is the most joyous season of the Church's year—the fifty days from Easter to Pentecost.

WHAT IS THE EASTER VIGIL?

The Easter Vigil is a celebration held at any time during the hours of darkness that precede the Easter sunrise (the name "vigil" means a night watch), and consists of a service of light, a liturgy of the word, a liturgy of Baptism and the liturgy of the Eucharist.

WHAT IS PENTECOST?

Pentecost is the Sunday seven weeks after Easter on which we celebrate the memory of the Holy Spirit's descent upon the Apostles. Pentecost is considered the "birthday" of the Church.

WHAT IS ORDINARY TIME?

Ordinary time is the season of the Church Year outside of the Advent-Christmas and Lent-Easter seasons, one part between the Christmas Season and Lent; and the other, between Pentecost and Advent.

WHAT IS A MISSAL?

A missal is a book containing all the Mass prayers, readings, etc., for the three-year Sunday cycle and two-year weekday cycle.

IN REGARD TO THE MASS, WHAT DO WE MEAN BY THE WORD "OPTION"?

Options are choices permitted by the Church to priests regarding the Mass. For example: he may say one of four Eucharistic Prayers.

CONFIRMATION

WHAT IS CONFIRMATION?

Confirmation is the sacrament in which the Holy Spirit comes to us in a special way to join us more closely to Jesus and His Church and to seal and strengthen us as Christ's witnesses.

"When the Paraclete comes,...
whom I myself will send from the Father—
he will bear witness on my behalf" (Jn. 15:26).* (See also: Acts 2:4; 8:14-17.)

WHO IS THE MINISTER OF CONFIRMATION?

The bishop is the ordinary minister of Confirmation. Bishops are the successors of the Apostles and leaders in the Church. In the Church's name the bishop sends confirmed Christians out on a mission — to spread the Faith by word and example. Priests may confirm in certain circumstances.

WHAT DOES "CONFIRM" MEAN?

To confirm means to strengthen. In Confirmation our faith is deepened and strengthened, and through this sacrament we are more perfectly bound to Christ and to His Church.

WHAT MAKES UP THE SIGN OF CONFIRMATION?

The sign of Confirmation is made up of anointing and words.

WHAT DOES THE ACTION OF CONFIRMING TELL US ABOUT THE SACRAMENT?

In the action of confirming, the anointing shows that strength and power are being received from the Holy Spirit. This anointing is done on the forehead, in the form of a cross, to show that we are proud of our Faith, and will witness to it even in the face of difficulties.

WHAT DO WE MEAN BY "ANOINTING"?

"Anointing" means "signing with oil." The blessed oil that is used is called chrism. It stands for strength — spiritual strength. The sweet-smelling balsam that it contains stands for freedom from sin and the spreading of goodness.

WHAT DO THE WORDS SIGNIFY?

The words signify that we are receiving the Holy Spirit in a special way, and are being sealed (marked) as Christ's witnesses.

WHAT DO WE MEAN WHEN WE SAY THAT A CHRISTIAN IS *SEALED* AS CHRIST'S WITNESS?

In Confirmation a Christian receives a second, spiritual seal which lasts forever. The first lasting spiritual seal was received at Baptism.

IS CONFIRMATION NECESSARY FOR THE ATTAINMENT OF SALVATION?

Confirmation is not absolutely necessary for the attainment of salvation, but it could be seriously wrong to neglect this sacrament because of the many valuable graces which it confers. Confirmation is also important for the growth of the Church.

HOW IS CONFIRMATION GIVEN?

The bishop extends his hands over the person and anoints the forehead in the form of a cross while saying: "Be sealed with the Gift of the Holy Spirit." The person being confirmed answers "Amen," meaning, "Let it be so." The Gift is the Holy Spirit Himself. He is the Gift of the Father and the Son to us.

WHAT IS A WITNESS TO CHRIST?

A witness to Christ is a person who tells or shows others something about Him.

HOW DO WE WITNESS TO CHRIST?

We witness to Christ by learning, living, loving, standing up for and sharing our Catholic Faith.

Our Catholic Faith means everything that we believe and do as Catholics.

WHO MAY RECEIVE CONFIRMATION?

Any baptized Catholic, who has not been confirmed, may receive Confirmation. The Church urges

Catholics to study their Faith well before receiving Confirmation, because a confirmed Catholic is expected to live up to his or her Faith. However, it is possible for even newly-baptized infants to be confirmed, and at times this is done.

HOW SHOULD A CATHOLIC PREPARE FOR CONFIRMATION?

A Catholic should prepare for Confirmation by studying the Catholic Faith, by praying, and witnessing to Christ.

WHAT IS THE PURPOSE OF A CONFIRMATION SPONSOR?

A Confirmation sponsor has the same duties as a baptismal godparent. The Church suggests that the baptismal godparent become the Confirmation sponsor also. However, another sponsor may be chosen, even one's own parent. A sponsor must be a good Catholic, already confirmed.

IS ANOTHER SAINT'S NAME TAKEN IN CONFIRMATION?

A Catholic may take another saint's name in Confirmation if he or she wishes.

WHAT ARE THE RIGHTS AND PRIVILEGES OF CONFIRMED CATHOLICS?

Confirmed Catholics have become full-fledged members of the Church. They have received spiritual strength and more actual graces to help them better witness to Christ. The confirmed have also grown in the graces and gifts first received in Baptism. This is indicated during the Confirmation ceremony when the Holy Spirit is called upon to come with His seven gifts.

WHAT ARE THE DUTIES OF CONFIRMED CATHOLICS?

Confirmed Catholics are to keep on learning about their Faith. They are to live it, love it, stand up for it, and share it as Christ's witnesses.

ANOINTING OF THE SICK

WHAT IS THE ANOINTING OF THE SICK?

The Anointing of the Sick is the sacrament by which Christ gives comfort and strength to the soul, and sometimes to the body, of someone who is dangerously ill due to sickness, injury, or old age.

WHO ACTS FOR JESUS IN THE ANOINTING OF THE SICK?

The priest acts for Jesus in the Anointing of the Sick. The Bible says:

If one of you is ill, he should send for the elders of the church, and they must anoint him with oil in the name of the Lord and pray over him. The prayer of faith will save the sick man and the Lord will raise him up again; and if he has committed any sins, he will be forgiven (Jas. 5:14-15).**

WHAT MAKES UP THE SIGN OF THE ANOINTING OF THE SICK?

The sign of the Anointing of the Sick is made up of anointing and words.

WHAT IS THE BLESSED OIL THAT IS USED IN THE ANOINTING?

The blessed oil that is used in the Anointing is called the oil of the sick. It stands for healing—chiefly spiritual healing, but also physical healing.

WHAT DO THE WORDS OF THE SACRAMENT OF ANOINTING SIGNIFY?

The words of the sacrament of Anointing signify that we are asking the Lord to give His strength, His healing, His grace.

WHO MAY RECEIVE THE ANOINTING OF THE SICK?

Any baptized person may receive the Anointing of the Sick who is capable of having sinned, and is dangerously ill due to sickness, injury, or old age.

WHAT DOES THIS SACRAMENT DO FOR A PERSON?

Through this sacrament, Christ:

—fortifies the sick person's soul with more grace and with the strength to resist temptations (for often temptations are strongest when one is physically weak);

—gives the sick person comfort to bear his or her sufferings bravely, and courage and consolation in the face of death;

—cleanses the soul of venial sin;

—even removes mortal sin, if the person would have wished forgiveness but is unable to make his confession.

Sometimes the sacrament also restores physical health, if that would be helpful for the sick person's salvation.

WHEN SHOULD A PERSON RECEIVE THE ANOINTING OF THE SICK?

A person should receive the Anointing of the Sick when he or she begins to be in danger of death due to sickness or old age. It is a good practice to ask the priest to visit sick members of the family in the case of serious illness, even though there is no apparent danger of death. Sick children, too, may receive this sacrament if they are old enough to be comforted by it.

The elderly who are in a weakened condition are also encouraged by the Church to receive the Anointing, even though no dangerous illness is present.

WHERE IS THE SACRAMENT OF THE ANOINTING RECEIVED?

The sacrament of the Anointing is usually received at home or in a hospital. At home, prepare a table, and cover it with a linen cloth in the sick room. On it you may place, if possible, a crucifix, two candles, and some holy water.

HOW IS THE ANOINTING OF THE SICK GIVEN?

The Anointing of the Sick is given by the priest who anoints the sick person on the forehead and hands, saying the appropriate prayers.

WHEN IS THE ANOINTING OF THE SICK GIVEN?

The Anointing of the Sick is usually given after the person has made his or her confession. However, it can even be given to someone who is unconscious.

WHAT IS NECESSARY TO RECEIVE THIS SACRAMENT WORTHILY?

To receive this sacrament worthily, one should be in the state of grace. For this reason it is customary to receive the sacrament of Penance first unless one is unconscious.

SHOULD A PRIEST BE CALLED, EVEN IF A PERSON IS APPARENTLY DEAD?

The priest *should* be called even if a person is apparently dead because the Anointing and absolution can be given conditionally for some time after apparent death.

WHAT ARE THE LAST SACRAMENTS?

The last sacraments are those received by a person who is seriously ill. They include Penance, the Anointing of the Sick, and Viaticum (Holy Eucharist).

WHAT OTHER SACRAMENTS ARE USUALLY RECEIVED BEFORE AND AFTER THE ANOINTING OF THE SICK?

Penance is usually received before the Anointing of the sick; then the Holy Eucharist.

HOW DOES THE PRIEST "MAKE A SICK CALL"?

The priest "makes a sick call" in this manner: he enters the house, gives everyone a greeting of peace, and then places the Blessed Sacrament on the table. All adore It. Then the priest sprinkles the sick person and the room with holy water, saying the prescribed prayer. The priest may then hear the sick person's confession. If sacramental confession is not part of the rite or if others are to receive Communion along with the sick person, the priest invites them to join in a penitential rite. A text from Scripture may then be read by one of those present or by the priest, who may explain the text. The Lord's Prayer follows. Then the priest distributes Holy Communion. A period of sacred silence may be observed. A concluding prayer and a blessing complete the Rite of Communion of the Sick.

At times *deacons* or *Eucharistic ministers* may visit the sick. Although they cannot celebrate the sacrament of Penance, they can distribute Holy Communion.

HOLY ORDERS

WHAT IS HOLY ORDERS?

Holy Orders is the sacrament through which men are given the grace and power to carry out the sacred duties of deacons, priests or bishops.

WHAT POWERS DO PRIESTS HAVE?

Priests have the God-given power to imitate Jesus in a special way by celebrating Mass and changing bread and wine into Jesus' Body and Blood. They also forgive sins in Jesus' name and bring His comfort in the Anointing of the Sick.

Besides this, priests can do everything that deacons can do. And in special cases, they can also administer Confirmation.

WHAT ARE THE DUTIES OF PARISH PRIESTS?

Parish priests, also called *secular* or *diocesan priests,* take care of the needs of the people in their parish, encouraging them to receive religious instruction and guidance about God's law and God's grace through the sacraments.

Parish priests are the helpers and co-workers of the bishops.

HOW MANY KINDS OF ORDINATION ARE THERE?

There are three kinds of ordination—to the diaconate, to the priesthood, to the episcopate. The diaconate means the position of a deacon; the episcopate means the position of a bishop.

WHO ACTS FOR JESUS IN CONFERRING HOLY ORDERS?

The bishop acts for Jesus in conferring Holy Orders.

WHO MAY RECEIVE HOLY ORDERS?

A man who is a good Catholic, has prepared himself by study, and has been accepted by the bishop may receive Holy Orders.

IS THE PRIESTHOOD A SPECIAL PRIVILEGE?

The priesthood is a special privilege. No one has a *right* to be ordained. A man is called to the priesthood by God through His Church. Therefore, ordination is God's gift to him, not his right.

HOW IS HOLY ORDERS GIVEN?

Holy Orders is given through the bishop's laying on of hands and his prayer that God may give the dignity of the priesthood to the man (or men) being ordained. When this takes place, the man receives more grace, the powers of the priesthood, and a third lasting spiritual seal—the character of a priest.

WHAT MAKES UP THE SIGN OF HOLY ORDERS?

The sign of Holy Orders is made up of the laying on of hands and a special prayer.

The bishop places his hands, palms downward, on the candidate's head to show the giving of the Holy Spirit, with His grace and power.

WHAT ARE THE RIGHTS AND PRIVILEGES OF THE PRIEST?

The priest has a right to lead the people whom he is to care for and to be respected by them. He acts for Jesus in the Mass and various sacraments.

A priest deserves the respect of his people because he has been dedicated to Christ in a very special way. A diocesan priest has to use his rights in obedience to his bishop. A priest in a religious order has to use his rights in obedience to his superiors.

WHAT ARE THE DUTIES OF PRIESTS?

Priests are to teach the people under their care, guide them in right living and bring them God's grace through the Mass and sacraments.

Priests have the great responsibility of teaching only what is taught by the Church (meaning the Pope and the bishops united *with* the Pope).

Because they are dedicated to Christ in a special way, priests bring Christ's love to His people and lead them to heaven.

WHAT IS THE FUNCTION OF DEACONS?

Deacons serve the people by baptizing, reading God's Word to the faithful, preaching, distributing Communion, giving Eucharistic Benediction, blessing couples who receive the sacrament of Matrimony, etc.

HOW MANY KINDS OF DEACONS ARE THERE?

There are two kinds of deacons. Men preparing for the priesthood are ordained as deacons before being or-

dained as priests. They remain deacons only for a time.
There are also permanent deacons. These are single and
married men who will remain deacons for the rest of
their lives.

MATRIMONY

WHAT IS MATRIMONY?

Matrimony is the sacrament through which a baptized man and a baptized woman join themselves for life in a lawful marriage and receive God's grace so that they may carry out their responsibilities.

HOW IS MARRIAGE A COVENANT?

As an agreement to be faithful to one another for life, marriage is a covenant.

WHAT IS THE PURPOSE OF MATRIMONY?

The purpose of Matrimony is twofold: the begetting and proper unbringing of children, and the mutual love and benefit of husband and wife. These two purposes are inseparable. In addition, Matrimony is a sacred sign recalling the perpetual love of Christ and His Church.

"Marriage and conjugal love are by their nature ordained toward the begetting and educating of children. Children are really the supreme gift of marriage and contribute very substantially to the welfare of their parents....

"Marriage to be sure is not instituted solely for procreation. Rather, its very nature as an unbreakable compact between persons, and the welfare of the children, both demand that the mutual love of the spouses be embodied in a rightly ordered manner, that it grow and ripen" (*Church in the Modern World,* no. 50).

WHEN DOES A CATHOLIC RECEIVE THE SACRAMENT OF MATRIMONY?

A Catholic receives the sacrament of Matrimony when he or she marries in Church or with the Church's permission.

WHAT IS THE "SIGN" OF MATRIMONY?

The sign of Matrimony is the exchange of vows (important promises) to love and be loyal to one another for a lifetime.

HOW IS MATRIMONY GIVEN?

Matrimony is given by the couple's exchange of marriage vows.

WHO ACTS FOR JESUS IN MATRIMONY?

Two persons act for Jesus in Matrimony, the man and woman who are receiving the sacrament. They give the sacrament of Matrimony to each other. The priest or deacon witnesses the sacrament and gives the couple God's blessing.

WHAT ARE THE EFFECTS OF THE SACRAMENT OF MATRIMONY?

The effects of the sacrament of Matrimony are growth in grace and a right to call upon God for all the help the couple will need in being loving and faithful for life, in bringing children into the world, and in raising their children as good Christian citizens.

WHAT ARE THE DUTIES OF MARRIED LIFE?

The duties of married life, in brief, are:
— lifelong love and fidelity;

—the begetting and proper rearing of children. Because of these God-given duties, artificial birth control, abortion and divorce with remarriage are sinful.

WHO MAY RECEIVE THE SACRAMENT OF MATRIMONY?

To receive the sacrament of Matrimony a person must be baptized and not already joined to someone else by Matrimony. The person must obey the marriage laws of the Church.

WHO MAY RECEIVE THE SACRAMENT OF MATRIMONY MORE THAN ONCE?

If someone received the sacrament of Matrimony and then the first partner dies, the living partner is free to receive Matrimony again.

A wife is bound to her husband as long as he lives. If her husband dies she is free to marry... (1 Cor. 7:39).*

WHAT ARE THE BANNS OF MARRIAGE?

The *banns* of marriage are three pulpit proclamations of the intended marriage of a couple at Masses on three successive Sundays or holy days of obligation. The purpose of the banns is to determine that there are no impediments to the coming marriage.

WHAT IS MEANT BY A MIXED MARRIAGE?

By a mixed marriage is meant the marriage of a Catholic to a non-Catholic.

ARE MIXED MARRIAGES PERMITTED?

Yes, mixed marriages are permitted (by a dispensation), but the Church does not encourage them. Catholics who enter mixed marriages must take great care to strengthen their faith, give good example and raise their children as Catholics.

WHY DOES THE CHURCH URGE CATHOLICS TO CONTRACT MARRIAGE ONLY WITH CATHOLICS?

The union of husband and wife in Matrimony is a sign of Christ's union with the Church. Married partners are called to perfect union of mind and communion of life, and this union can be broken or weakened when differences of opinion or disagreement touch on matters of religious truths and convictions. Religion is such a vital force that when a couple cannot share it, they feel something missing from their union. The greater the difference in religious beliefs, the greater the potential for problems.

WHY IS THE SACRAMENT OF MARRIAGE UNBREAKABLE?

Marriage is unbreakable because God wills it so (cf. Mk. 10:2-12). The "unbreakableness" of marriage, called *indissolubility,* is for the good of the couple, their children and the whole of society.

DOES THE CHURCH EVER PERMIT A SEPARATION?

In cases which become unbearable, the Church allows the partners of a valid marriage a separation, but without the right to marry again.

WHAT ARE SOME REASONS FOR THE CHURCH TO GRANT A SEPARATION?

The reason for perpetual separation arises from adultery of one of the partners. Other causes which permit the injured partner to seek a temporary or indefinite separation are: criminal or shameful conduct, the education of the children in schism or heresy, grave danger to soul and body.

WHAT IS DIVORCE?

Divorce is an evil which attempts to break the unity of the marriage bond that can never be broken except by death. Jesus said:

"Have you not read that the creator from the beginning *made them male and female* and that he said: *This is why a man must leave father and mother, and cling to his wife, and the two become one body?* They are no longer two, therefore, but one body. So then, what God has united, man must not divide" (Mt. 19:5-6).**

IS DIVORCE EVER PERMITTED?

Divorce with remarriage is never permitted by the Church. The Church might permit a couple to obtain a civil divorce for legal reasons, but in God's eyes this couple is only separated. Neither may marry again while his or her spouse is still living.

"Everyone who divorces his wife and marries another commits adultery. The man who marries a woman divorced from her husband likewise commits adultery" (Lk. 16:18).*

WHAT ARE SOME NEEDS OF TODAY'S DIVORCED CATHOLICS?

Today's divorced Catholics need:

—special guidance not to become bitter, not to talk about "rules of the Church," when these are the rules of Christ;

—guidance in keeping with the eternal teachings of Christ to overcome feelings of loneliness and desolation;

—encouragement to keep close to the sacraments, especially Holy Communion;

—encouragement never to enter into an invalid marriage, because that cuts one off from receiving the life-giving and life-sustaining sacraments.

WHAT IS RECOMMENDED FOR CATHOLICS LIVING IN AN INVALID MARRIAGE?

For Catholics living in an invalid marriage, the religious problems are greater and the need for counseling is also greater. Such Catholics must never lose hope or lose sight of salvation. They should by all means remain faithful to Sunday Mass, parish life and personal prayer. It is a difficult way to live and reach salvation—but the mercy of God is great, especially to the contrite of heart.

WHAT IS AN ANNULMENT?

A Decree of Nullity or annulment is a decision by Church authorities that an apparently valid marriage between two baptized persons can be declared null because of a fatal flaw. These flaws, unknown to one or both parties, or concealed by one or the other, make the marriage no marriage from the start. Church "tribunals" study each case and, where proper, give a Decree of Nullity—commonly called an annulment.

WHAT IS ADULTERY?

Adultery is the sin of sexual intercourse between a married person and someone who is not his or her married partner.

IS THERE AN ACCEPTABLE METHOD OF BIRTH CONTROL?

The Church recognizes natural methods of birth control (as opposed to artificial), because these do not directly block God's creative action. (Information about natural methods may be obtained from Catholic natural family planning groups.)

WHAT IS NECESSARY TO RECEIVE THE SACRA-MENT OF MATRIMONY WORTHILY?

To receive the sacrament of Matrimony worthily it is necessary to be free from mortal sin, to know and understand the duties of married life, and to obey the laws of the Church concerning marriage.

HOW SHOULD CATHOLICS PREPARE FOR MAR-RIAGE?

In preparing for marriage, young people should
—study the beauty, nobility and duties of married life;
—practice virtue—especially chastity;
—pray for the wisdom to choose the right partner for this lifelong contract;
—seek also the advice of their parents and the priest to whom they usually go to confession;
—receive the sacraments of Penance and Holy Eucharist often.

SACRAMENT OF PENANCE

WHAT IS THE SACRAMENT OF PENANCE?

Penance is the sacrament of God's loving forgiveness by which we are set free from sin, from its eternal punishment, and from at least some of its temporal punishment. This sacrament also helps us to grow in God's grace. It strengthens us to avoid sin and to lead holier lives.

FROM WHOM DO WE RECEIVE THE GIFT OF THE SACRAMENT OF PENANCE?

We receive the gift of the sacrament of Penance from Jesus Himself who gave the apostles the power to forgive sins with these words:

"Receive the Holy Spirit.
If you forgive men's sins,
they are forgiven them;
if you hold them bound,
they are held bound" (Jn. 20:22-23).*

HOW DO WE KNOW THAT GOD IS WILLING TO FORGIVE SINS?

We know that God is willing to forgive sins because in the Gospel Jesus has told us many times and in many ways that God is willing to forgive our sins. For example, He said: "The Son of Man has come to search out and save what was lost" (Lk. 19:10).*

WHAT MAKES UP THE SIGN OF PENANCE?

The sign of Penance is made up of three "acts of the penitent," plus the words of the priest.

WHAT IS A PENITENT?

A penitent is someone who is sorry for his or her sins. The penitent's three acts are contrition (sorrow), confession and satisfaction (making up for the harm done when possible, and doing or saying the penance given by the priest. We also may perform or say other penances beyond what is required.).

HOW IS THE SACRAMENT OF PENANCE GIVEN?

The sacrament of Penance is given when we go to confession with sorrow for sin, accept the penance that the priest gives, and receive the priest's absolution: "...I absolve you from your sins in the name of the Father, and of the Son, and of the Holy Spirit."

As when receiving the Eucharist and Confirmation, we answer, "Amen."

WHAT FIVE STEPS ARE NECESSARY FOR RECEIVING THE SACRAMENT OF PENANCE WORTHILY?

The five steps necessary for receiving the sacrament of Penance worthily are: examination of conscience, contrition, resolution, confession and acceptance of the penance. The sorrow of the penitent has to come from love of God, fear of His punishments, or hatred of sin itself.

WHAT IS PERFECT CONTRITION?

Perfect contrition is sorrow for sin especially because sin displeases God, who is all-good and loving, and deserves all our love.

WHAT IS IMPERFECT CONTRITION?

Imperfect contrition is sorrow for sin for reasons that are good but not the very best—for example, more out of fear than out of love.

WHAT IS THE SEAL OF CONFESSION?

The "seal of confession" is the most solemn obligation of a priest to keep secret what has been revealed to him in confession.

MAY A PRIEST EVER BREAK THIS "SEAL"?

The priest may never break this seal even to save his own life.

SHOULD WE EVER SPEAK OF WHAT WE HEARD OR SAID IN CONFESSION?

With regard to overhearing someone else's confession, we are strictly bound to secrecy; regarding our own confession we are not. However, it is better not to talk about the advice given, the penance, etc.

SHOULD WE EVER BE SO EMBARRASSED THAT WE DO NOT GO TO CONFESSION?

We should never be so embarrassed that we do not go to confession. We must remember that the priest is Christ's representative and that he is bound by the seal of confession never to reveal anything told to him in the confessional. Also, we are free to confess to any priest.

CAN EVERY SIN BE FORGIVEN?

Yes, every sin can be forgiven through the sacrament of Penance. Jesus said to the Apostles:

"Whatever you bind on earth shall be considered bound in heaven; whatever you loose on earth shall be considered loosed in heaven" (Mt. 16:19).**

DOES THE PRIEST EVER REFUSE ABSOLUTION?

The priest can refuse absolution to the penitent if the person is not really sorry for his serious sins or has no intention of correcting himself. Unless there is true sorrow, there is no forgiveness.

WHO MAY RECEIVE THE SACRAMENT OF PENANCE?

Any Catholic who has committed sin may receive the sacrament of Penance.

WHAT DOES ABSOLUTION MEAN?

Absolution means "releasing." When the priest absolves us, we are released from our sins—set free from them.

He who conceals his faults will not prosper,
he who confesses and renounces them will find mercy
(Prv. 28:13).**

WHAT IS A PENANCE?

A penance is something done or accepted to make up for sin. The Bible says:

"Come back to me with all your heart,
fasting, weeping, mourning" (Jl. 2:12).**

WHO ACTS FOR JESUS IN THE SACRAMENT OF PENANCE?

The priest acts for Jesus in the sacrament of Penance. When we confess our sins to the priest, we are confessing them to Jesus. And Jesus forgives us through the priest.

WHO IS A CONFESSOR?

The word "confessor" may have two meanings. It can mean a priest who hears confessions, or it can mean a saint, other than a martyr, who witnessed to ("confessed") the Faith.

WHY DO WE TELL OUR SINS TO THE PRIEST?

We tell our sins to the priest because he has to know what our sins are in order to forgive them in Christ's name. St. John says:

...If we acknowledge our sins,
then God who is faithful and just
will forgive our sins and purify us
from everything that is wrong (1 Jn. 1:9).**

CAN A PERSON CONFESS HIS SINS WITH THE INTENTION OF COMMITTING THEM AGAIN?

A person cannot confess his sins with the intention of committing them again. No sin is forgiven by God unless there is supernatural sorrow for it (even imperfect sorrow, such as fear of divine punishment) and a firm resolution not to commit it again.

ARE THERE TIMES WHEN A PERSON MUST CONFESS HIS SINS TO A PRIEST, THAT IS, GO TO CONFESSION?

A person must confess his sins to a priest, that is, go to confession if he has committed a mortal or serious sin. A mortal sin can be forgiven even before confession if a person has perfect (pure) sorrow for having offended our loving God. But he or she must still go to confession before receiving Holy Communion. If we have committed mortal sin, we should go to confession soon.

HOW OFTEN MUST WE RECEIVE THE SACRAMENT OF PENANCE?

The Church commands us to receive the sacrament of Penance (confession) at least once a year if we have serious sins. Good Catholics try to go once a month or even weekly, if possible. All mortal sins must be confessed, but we may also confess venial sins and faults. In other words, all that which keeps us from drawing closer to God is subject matter for confession.

IS IT BENEFICIAL TO RECEIVE THE SACRAMENT OF PENANCE FREQUENTLY, EVEN IF WE HAVE COMMITTED ONLY VENIAL SINS?

It is an excellent practice to receive the sacrament of Penance frequently. Even if we have no serious sins to confess, this sacrament helps us to realize that *all* sin offends God. It helps us to know and correct our faults, to grow in grace and love of God and neighbor, and to strengthen our will power and self-control. In short, frequent reception of the sacrament of Penance helps us to become better Catholics.

WHEN MAY A "GENERAL ABSOLUTION" BE GIVEN?

In certain rare cases, a "general absolution" may be given to a group without individual confession. As always, the penitents must be sorry and intend not to sin again. After the absolution, they may receive Communion, but they are still obliged to tell their mortal sins in confession within a year.

WHAT ARE THE RIGHTS AND PRIVILEGES OF ONE WHO HAS RECEIVED THE SACRAMENT OF PENANCE?

The rights and privileges of one who has received the sacrament of Penance consist in this: A person who was in mortal sin may now receive the Eucharist and other sacraments. He or she has been reconciled with God and the Church.

WHAT ARE THE DUTIES OF ONE WHO HAS RECEIVED THE SACRAMENT OF PENANCE?

One who has received the sacrament of Penance must say or do the penance given by the priest, avoid everything that would lead to sin, and make up as much as possible for the harm done.

How the harm is to be made up for is explained under various commandments, such as the seventh and eighth.

WHAT ARE THE EFFECTS OF THIS SACRAMENT?
When we receive the sacrament of Penance worthily, the effects are the following:
—our sins are forgiven
—our soul is restored to the state of grace (if we had committed mortal sins), or we grow in sanctifying grace (if we committed venial sins);
—we are set free from all the eternal punishment and at least some of the temporal punishment due to our sins;
—we receive the sacramental grace of Penance, which strengthens us to avoid sin in the future;
—we receive the help to lead better lives.

HOW DOES ONE EXAMINE HIS CONSCIENCE?
One examines his conscience by recalling what wrong he has done in thoughts, words and actions as well as the duties accomplished poorly or not carried out at all. As a help, the ten commandments can be recalled one by one, as well as the special duties of Catholic Christians and one's own particular duties.

In addition, some questions like the following will help us:

1. What is my attitude toward the sacrament of God's mercy, the sacrament of Penance?

2. Do I want my sins forgiven, so that I can begin a new life and deepen my friendship with God?

3. Did I deliberately conceal serious sins in past confessions through fear or shame? Now I want to tell them sincerely, trusting that God will forgive me as He forgave the Prodigal Son.

4. Did I perform the penance I was given during my last confession? Did I make up for any injuries I caused others?

5. Have I really been trying to become a better Catholic, the way the Gospel teaches?

How Much Do I Love God?

Do I love God and prove it by obeying His Ten Commandments?

Do I think about pleasing God, and try to live every day as well as I can?

Do I *believe* in God and trust Him? Or am I much more concerned about the things of this world?

Do I accept what the Catholic Church teaches?

Do I try to grow in knowledge and love of my Catholic Faith?

Am I courageous in professing my faith in God and the Church?

Am I proud to be a Catholic, willing to be known as one?

Do I say morning and evening prayers?

Do I turn to God often during the day, especially when I am tempted?

Do I love and reverence God's name? Did I ever take His name in vain?

Did I blaspheme or swear falsely?

Did I show disrespect for our Lady and the saints?

Do I assist at Mass with attention and devotion on Sundays and holydays?

Have I fulfilled the precept of Communion during the Easter Season?

Are there "false gods" in my life: money, clothes, superstition, desire for popularity, that actually mean more to me than God does?

How Much Do I Love My Neighbor?

Do I really love my neighbor, or do I use people for my own ends? Do I do to them what I would *not* want done to myself?

Have I given bad example by my words or actions?

Do I contribute to the happiness of every member of my family?

Am I obedient and respectful to my parents?

If I am permitted, am I *willing* to share my possessions with those who have less, or do I look down on them?

Do I share in the apostolic and charitable works of the parish?

Do I pray for the needs of the Church and the world?

In school and at home, am I hardworking and conscientious in fulfilling my duties?

Am I truthful and fair? Did I ever damage another's good name?

Have I ever damaged another person's property or possessions? Have I stolen?

Have I quarreled? Made insulting remarks? Been angry?

Do I harbor hatred and a thirst for revenge?

How Is My Personal Growth in the Christian Life?

Do I think about heaven and hope for eternal life with God?

Do I pray often? Do I read God's Word, the Bible, and reflect on it?

Do I receive the sacraments of Penance and Holy Eucharist regularly?

Am I pure in my thoughts, words, desires, actions?

Do I keep away from indecent literature, movies, dangerous companions, etc.?

Do I know how to make small acts of self-denial?

Do I really try to control my vices? To admit my mistakes? Or have I been proud, boastful, demanding on others?

Am I lazy? Do I waste a lot of time?

Do I use my talents and time to help others know Jesus?

Am I patient in accepting disappointments and sorrows?

PERSONAL SIN

WHAT IS SIN?
Sin is disobedience to God's law. People begin to commit sin when they reach what is called the "age of reason" (usually around seven or earlier). The severely retarded cannot sin and so do not need the sacrament of Penance.

WHAT IS ACTUAL SIN?
Actual sin is personal sin, sin which we ourselves commit.

ARE THERE DIFFERENT KINDS OF PERSONAL OR ACTUAL SIN?
There are two kinds of personal or actual sin, mortal and venial.

WHAT IS MORTAL SIN?
Mortal sin is a serious offense against God's law.

HOW CAN WE KNOW IF A SIN IS MORTAL?

A sin is mortal if:

—before or while committing it the person clearly knows (or thinks) that it is something seriously wrong. The sinner is aware of the serious wrong if at the time he foresees the sin will follow, or knows or at least suspects that the action is grievously sinful.

—it regards a serious matter. That which is seriously sinful, wrong or evil is known to be such from Sacred Scripture, Tradition, the teachings of the Church or the kind of sin itself.

—the person freely gives full consent to it. A sinner fully consents to do wrong when he freely chooses to do evil, although he is entirely free not to do it.

WHAT SHOULD A PERSON DO IF HE OR SHE HAS COMMITTED A MORTAL SIN?

A person who has committed a mortal sin should say a prayer of perfect sorrow with the intention of going to confession soon. This restores sanctifying grace. But this person may not receive Communion until he has gone to confession.

ARE THERE ANY REQUIREMENTS FOR CONFESSING MORTAL SINS?

The requirements for confessing mortal sins are: a person should say what kind of sins they were and—as far as possible—tell how many times these sins were committed, as well as any circumstances that might alter their nature.

CAN A PERSON RIGHTLY SAY THAT GOD IS RESPONSIBLE FOR PERSONAL SIN SINCE IT IS GOD WHO PERMITS CERTAIN TEMPTATIONS?

A person can never rightly say that God is responsible for his personal sin because God is all-good and all-holy, and for everyone who prays, God always provides sufficient grace to overcome temptations. The Bible says:

Say not: "It was God's doing that I fell away";
   for what he hates he does not do.
Say not: "It was he who set me astray";
   for he has no need of wicked man (Sir. 15:11-12).*

WHAT IS THE FALSE THEORY CALLED "SITUATION ETHICS"?

Situation ethics teaches that there is no fixed moral code given to human beings by the Creator. It holds that individuals must make moral choices (choices about right and wrong) according to a particular situation—that is, what is right or best in this moment *for me.* This false theory permits gravely sinful actions, and leads people who follow it down the road to despair because the human mind cannot long be pressured into calling gravely sinful matters "slight."

WHAT IS MEANT BY THE ABUSE OF THE SO-CALLED "FUNDAMENTAL OPTION"?*

By this abuse is meant that if a good man does something gravely sinful, that particular action is not gravely sinful for him. One gravely sinful act (a mortal sin) is not enough to separate him from God; a series of

---

*See: *Declaration on Sexual Ethics,* no. 10.

gravely forbidden acts would be required. This teaching is false and is not what the Church teaches regarding sin or man's free will and personal responsibility for his actions.

WHAT IS A VENIAL SIN?

A sin is venial when one of the conditions for a mortal sin is missing. For example, the thought, desire, word, action or omission is wrong but not seriously so, or it is seriously wrong but a person does not clearly see this, or does not fully consent to it.

DOES VENIAL SIN HARM US?

Venial sin harms us by making us care less about God and our Catholic Faith. It makes us weaker when faced with serious sin, and makes us deserving of God's punishments on this earth and in purgatory.

SHOULD WE AVOID VENIAL SINS?

We should avoid venial sins because even though they do not destroy the life of grace, they are an offense to God, and they weaken our friendship with Him. They also dispose us to mortal sin and merit for us some temporal punishment either in this life or in the next.

WHAT ARE SINS OF OMISSION?

Sins of omission are the failure to do something one should have done.

ARE SINS OF OMISSION MORTAL OR VENIAL?

Sins of omission may be mortal or venial depending upon what we have failed to do.

WHAT ARE THE CHIEF REASONS WHY PEOPLE COMMIT SIN?

The chief reasons why people commit sin may be found in the seven capital sins.

WHAT ARE THE SEVEN CAPITAL SINS?

The seven capital sins are pride, covetousness, lust, anger, gluttony, envy and sloth. Pride is inordinate or uncontrolled self-esteem. Covetousness is an excessive desire for worldly goods. Lust is uncontrolled sexual desire. Anger is a strong, uncontrolled passion of displeasure. Gluttony is excessive indulgence in food and/or drink. Envy is sorrow at another's good fortune. Sloth is spiritual, mental or physical laziness which causes a person to neglect his duties.

FOR WHAT WILL GOD REWARD US?

God will reward us for all our victories over temptation and sin, for all our good deeds and sacrifices done out of love for Him, for all our efforts to grow closer to Him.

...Faith is dead if it is separated from good deeds (Jas. 2:26).**

WHAT ARE THE FOUR SINS THAT CRY TO HEAVEN FOR VENGEANCE?

The four sins that cry to heaven for vengeance are:
— voluntary murder
— sodomy
— taking advantage of the poor
— defrauding the workingman of his wages.

WHAT DO WE MEAN BY THE FOUR LAST THINGS?

The four last things are death, judgment, heaven and hell.

WHAT ARE THE SIX SINS AGAINST THE HOLY SPIRIT?

The six sins against the Holy Spirit are:

1. despair of one's salvation
2. presumption of saving oneself without merit or repentance
3. resisting the known truth
4. envy of the graces received by others
5. obstinacy in one's sins
6. final impenitence.

INDULGENCES*

WHAT IS AN INDULGENCE?

An indulgence is the removal of some or all of the temporal punishment for sin that we should have had to suffer on earth or in purgatory.

HOW MANY KINDS OF INDULGENCES ARE THERE?

There are two kinds of indulgences, *plenary* and *partial.*

WHAT IS A PLENARY INDULGENCE?

A plenary indulgence is the removal of all the punishment—called temporal punishment—a person would have had to suffer in purgatory for remitted sins.

----

*See: Apostolic Constitution on Indulgences *(Indulgentiarum Doctrina),* Pope Paul VI, St. Paul Editions.

WHAT IS A PARTIAL INDULGENCE?

A partial indulgence is the shortening or lessening of some of the temporal punishment due to forgiven sin. It can be acquired more than once a day, and can also be applied to the poor souls in purgatory.

WHAT IS THE TEMPORAL PUNISHMENT DUE TO OUR SINS?

The temporal punishment due to our sins is the punishment which one is obliged to endure for a time, either in this life or in purgatory, for sins already forgiven.

WHY DO WE HAVE ADDITIONAL "PUNISHMENT" FOR FORGIVEN SINS?

We have additional "punishment" for forgiven sins because of the seriousness and evil of sin; also because of the infinite majesty of the One offended, God.

HOW IS THE CHURCH ABLE TO GRANT INDULGENCES?

The Church is able to grant indulgences because she dispenses from her spiritual treasury "the infinite and inexhaustible value the expiation and the merits of Christ our Lord have before God, offered as they were so that all mankind could be set free from sin and attain communion with the Father" (Apostolic Constitution on Indulgences, no. 5).

HOW DOES THE CHURCH BY MEANS OF INDULGENCES REMIT THE TEMPORAL PUNISHMENT DUE TO SIN?

The Church takes away the temporal punishment due to sin by giving to us from her treasure of grace part

of the infinite satisfaction of Jesus. (See: Rom. 5:15-21;
1 Tm. 2:5-6; 1 Jn. 2:1-2.)

CAN WE GAIN INDULGENCES FOR OTHERS BE-SIDES OURSELVES?

We cannot gain indulgences for other living persons, but we can gain them for the souls in purgatory.

In the Old Testament, Judas Maccabaeus

"...had this atonement sacrifice offered for the dead, so
that they might be released from their sin" (2 Mc. 12:45).**

DOES THE CHURCH'S "TREASURY" ALSO IN-CLUDE THE GOOD WORKS OF THE BLESSED VIRGIN MARY AND ALL THE SAINTS?

The Church's "treasury" also "includes the truly
immense, unfathomable and ever pristine value before
God of the prayers and good works of the Blessed
Virgin Mary and all the saints, who following in the
footsteps of Christ the Lord and by His grace have sanc-
tified their lives and fulfilled the mission entrusted to
them by the Father" (Ap. Const. on Indulgences, no. 5).

WHY DOES THE CHURCH GRANT INDULGENCES?

The Church grants indulgences as one of the
"various ways of applying the fruits of the Lord's
redemption to the individual faithful and of leading them
to cooperate in the salvation of their brothers..." (Ap.
Const. on Indulgences, no. 6).

IS THE ONLY PURPOSE OF INDULGENCES TO HELP THE FAITHFUL TO EXPIATE THE PUNISHMENT DUE TO SIN?

Besides helping the faithful to expiate the punishment due to sin, the Church is also "urging them to per-

form works of piety, penitence and charity—particularly those which lead to growth in faith and which favor the common good" (Ap. Const. on Indulgences, no. 8).

IS BELIEF IN INDULGENCES CONFIRMED BY THE TEACHING AUTHORITY OF THE CHURCH?

Belief in indulgences has been confirmed by the teaching authority of the Church who "teaches and establishes that the use of indulgences must be preserved because it is supremely salutary for the Christian people and authoritatively approved by the sacred councils; and it condemns with anathema those who maintain the uselessness of indulgences or deny the power of the Church to grant them" (Apostolic Constitution on Indulgences, quoting Denz. 1835).

ARE THE INDULGENCES GAINED BY THE LIVING APPLICABLE TO THE DECEASED?

Indulgences gained by the living are applicable to the deceased, and when offered "in suffrage for the dead, they cultivate charity in an excellent way and while raising their minds to heaven, they bring a wiser order into the things of this world" (Apostolic Constitution on Indulgences, no. 8).

HOW OFTEN CAN A PLENARY INDULGENCE BE ACQUIRED?

A plenary indulgence can be acquired only once a day, unless at the point of death.

WHAT IS REQUIRED TO GAIN A PLENARY INDULGENCE?

To gain a plenary indulgence "it is necessary to perform the work to which the indulgence is attached and to fulfill three conditions: sacramental confession,

Eucharistic Communion and prayer for the intentions of
the Supreme Pontiff. It is further required that all at-
tachment to sin, even venial sin, be absent" (Norm
no. 7).

WHAT HAPPENS IF THE ABOVE REQUIREMENTS FOR A PLENARY INDULGENCE ARE NOT FULFILLED?

If the above requirements for a plenary indulgence
are not fulfilled, the indulgence will be only partial (cf.
Norm no. 7).

WHEN MAY THE CONDITIONS FOR RECEIVING A PLENARY INDULGENCE BE MET?

"The three conditions may be fulfilled several days
before or after the performance of the prescribed work;
nevertheless it is fitting that Communion be received
and the prayers for the intentions of the Supreme Pontiff be said the same day the work is performed" (Norm
no. 8).

WHEN MUST THE SACRAMENT OF PENANCE BE RECEIVED IN ORDER TO GAIN A PLENARY INDULGENCE?

The sacrament of Penance may be received even
several days before acquiring the indulgence. In fact:
"A single sacramental confession suffices for gaining
several plenary indulgences, but Communion must be
received and prayers for the Supreme Pontiff's intentions recited for the gaining of each plenary indulgence"
(Norm no. 9).

HOW IS THE CONDITION OF PRAYING FOR THE SUPREME PONTIFF MET?

"The condition of praying for the Supreme
Pontiff's intentions is fully satisfied by reciting one 'Our

Father' and one 'Hail Mary'; nevertheless the individual faithful are free to recite any other prayer according to their own piety and devotion toward the Supreme Pontiff'' (Norm no. 10).

CAN BISHOPS GRANT A PLENARY INDULGENCE TO THEIR FAITHFUL WHO LIVE WHERE IT IS IMPOSSIBLE OR AT LEAST VERY DIFFICULT FOR THEM TO RECEIVE THE SACRAMENTS OF CONFESSION AND COMMUNION?

Bishops ''can grant to the faithful over whom they exercise authority in accordance with the law, and who live in places where it is impossible or at least very difficult for them to receive the sacraments of Confession and Communion, permission to acquire a plenary indulgence without Confession and Communion provided they are sorry for their sins and have the intentions of receiving these sacraments as soon as possible'' (Norm no. 11).

CAN A PLENARY INDULGENCE BE ACQUIRED ON ALL SOULS DAY, NOVEMBER 2?

''A plenary indulgence applicable only to the dead can be acquired in all churches and public oratories —and in semi-public oratories by those who have the right to use them—on November 2'' (Norm no. 15).

WHAT KIND OF AN INDULGENCE DO THE FAITHFUL RECEIVE WHO USE WITH DEVOTION AN OBJECT OF PIETY PROPERLY BLESSED BY ANY PRIEST?

''The faithful who use with devotion an object of piety (crucifix, cross, rosary, scapular or medal) properly blessed by any priest, can acquire a partial indulgence'' (Norm no. 17).

WHEN CAN AN OBJECT OF PIETY, AS MENTIONED IN THE PREVIOUS QUESTIONS, BE USED TO ACQUIRE A PLENARY INDULGENCE?

An object of piety if blessed by the Pope or bishop can be used to acquire a plenary indulgence "on the feast of the holy apostles Peter and Paul, provided they [those acquiring the plenary indulgence] also make a profession of faith using any legitimate formula" (Norm no. 17).

WHAT ARE SACRAMENTALS?

WHAT ARE SACRAMENTALS?

Sacramentals are holy things or actions with which the Church asks God to grant us favors. Scripture speaks of how God told the Chosen People to use material things such as ashes and water in the Old Law. (See: Jn. 3:14-15; Nm. 19:1-22; Nm. 21:4-9.)

DO SACRAMENTALS OBTAIN BLESSINGS AND FAVORS FROM GOD?

Sacramentals do obtain favors from God through the prayers of God's People offered for those who make use of them, and because of the devotion they inspire.

WHAT ARE THE MAIN KINDS OF SACRAMENTALS?

The main kinds of sacramentals are:

—the blessing given by a priest, bishop or the Pope.

"Whatever house you go into, let your first words be, 'Peace to this house!' And if a man of peace lives there, your peace will go and rest on him; if not, it will come back to you" (Lk. 10:5-6).**

—exorcisms for the removal of evil spirits.

Jesus now called the Twelve together and gave them power and authority to overcome all demons and to cure diseases (Lk. 9:1).*

—blessed devotional objects.

WHICH BLESSED OBJECTS OF DEVOTION ARE MOST COMMONLY USED AMONG CATHOLICS?

Blessed objects of devotion most commonly used among Catholics are rosaries, relics, medals, crucifixes, scapulars, pictures of Jesus, Mary, the saints, ashes, palms, candles.

DO SACRAMENTALS BRING GOOD LUCK?

Sacramentals should never be considered good luck charms, nor made the objects of superstition. For example, one cannot lead an immoral life because he believes that the scapular or medal he wears will grant him the grace of conversion before he dies.

WHAT IS A SCAPULAR?

A scapular is two small pieces of cloth, fastened by strings and worn around the neck in front and in back. The most common scapular honors Mary as Our Lady of Mount Carmel. A scapular medal may be worn in place of a scapular.

WHAT ARE BLESSINGS?

Blessings are words and actions by which a thing or person is placed under the care of God.

WHAT IS HOLY WATER?

Holy water is water blessed by a priest in order to give God's blessing to those who use it.

WHY DO WE MAKE THE SIGN OF THE CROSS WITH HOLY WATER UPON ENTERING AND LEAVING CHURCH?

We make the sign of the cross with holy water upon entering and leaving Church to remind ourselves of our baptismal commitment and promises.

HOW ARE SACRAMENTALS DIFFERENT FROM SACRAMENTS?

Sacramentals differ from sacraments in this manner: the sacraments *give* grace directly through the actions of Jesus, while sacramentals help us indirectly to obtain God's grace.

WHAT IS THE PURPOSE OF BLESSED CANDLES?

Blessed candles are lit to witness to our devotion to Jesus who is light and life with His grace.

WHAT IS THE PURPOSE OF BLESSED ASHES?

Blessed ashes are used especially on Ash Wednesday, the first day of Lent. A cross is traced with ashes on our forehead as a reminder to live a good life and do penance because one day we will die.

WHAT IS THE PURPOSE OF CRUCIFIXES, MEDALS, SCAPULARS, RELIGIOUS STATUES AND HOLY PICTURES?

Crucifixes, medals, scapulars, religious statues and holy pictures have as their purpose to serve as reminders for us of our holy Faith, heaven, etc.

DO WE PRAY TO RELIGIOUS STATUES AND PICTURES?

We do not pray *to* the religious statues and pictures themselves. Instead, we pray to the person in heaven whom the statue or picture represents.

WHAT IS THE PURPOSE OF THE ROSARY BEADS?

The rosary beads are "prayer beads" which, when blessed, are enriched with many indulgences for reciting the prescribed prayers. These beads are used to recite the "Gospel prayer" made up of Our Father's, Hail Mary's and Glory's, in which we think about important events in the lives of Jesus and Mary. (See Prayer pages at the beginning of this catechism for instructions on how to say the rosary.)

The Ten Commandments

WHAT IS CONSCIENCE?

WHAT IS CONSCIENCE?
Conscience is a practical judgment (decision) that something is right or wrong according to the law and will of God.

WHAT IS NECESSARY TO HAVE A CORRECT CONSCIENCE?
To have a correct conscience one first needs to know God's law (the natural law for all men, written down in the Ten Commandments and made more perfect by Jesus), the laws of the Church and also his or her particular duties as a Catholic. Then one's conscience will really express what is right or wrong in a particular situation.

HOW ELSE MAY CONSCIENCE BE DEFINED?
"Conscience is the most secret core and sanctuary of a man. There he is alone with God, whose voice echoes in his depths.... In the depths of his conscience, man detects a law which he does not impose upon himself, but which holds him to obedience. Always summoning him to love good and avoid evil, the voice of conscience can when necessary speak to his heart more specifically: do this, shun that. For man

has in his heart a law written by God; to obey it is the very dignity of man; according to it he will be judged" (Pastoral Constitution on the Church in the Modern World, no. 16).

WHAT ARE THE COMMANDMENTS OF GOD?

The Commandments of God are these ten:

I am the Lord your God:

1. You shall not have strange gods before me.
2. You shall not take the name of the Lord your God in vain.
3. Remember to keep holy the Sabbath day.
4. Honor your father and your mother.
5. You shall not kill.
6. You shall not commit adultery.
7. You shall not steal.
8. You shall not bear false witness against your neighbor.
9. You shall not covet your neighbor's wife.
10. You shall not covet your neighbor's goods (cf. Ex. 20:1-17).

CAN THE TEN COMMANDMENTS OF GOD BE OBSERVED?

The Ten Commandments of God can be observed, all of them and always, even in the strongest temptations, with the grace that God never denies to one who invokes Him from the heart.

If you choose you can keep the commandments;
   it is loyalty to do his will (Sir. 15:15).*

And St. John assures us:

...His commandments are not burdensome (1 Jn. 5:3).*

ARE WE OBLIGED TO KEEP THE COMMANDMENTS OF GOD?

Yes, we are obliged to keep the commandments of God, because they are laid on us by Him who is our supreme Master, who revealed them, and they are indicated by our nature and by sound reason. Rather than doing away with the commandments, Jesus came to make them more perfect.

Whoever fulfills and teaches these commands shall be great in the kingdom of God (Mt. 5:19).*

HOW ARE THE TEN COMMANDMENTS DIVIDED?

The Ten Commandments are divided in this manner: the first three show us the way to love God; the other seven, how to love our neighbor.

WHAT DOES ST. PAUL SAY ABOUT THE TEN COMMANDMENTS?

About the Ten Commandments St. Paul says:

The commandments, "You shall not commit adultery; you shall not murder; you shall not steal; you shall not covet," and any other commandment there may be are all summed up in this, "You shall love your neighbor as yourself" (Rom. 13:9).*

FIRST COMMANDMENT

WHAT IS THE FIRST COMMANDMENT?

The first commandment is:

"You shall not have other gods besides me" (Dt. 5:7).*
"You shall not follow other gods...for the Lord, your God,...is a jealous God" (Dt. 6:14-15).*

WHAT ARE WE OBLIGED TO DO BY THE FIRST COMMANDMENT?

By the first commandment, we are obliged to love God above all things and adore Him alone. To adore God means to render Him the worship due Him as our sovereign Creator and Lord, avoiding the sins of idolatry and sacrilege.

"You shall do homage to the Lord your God;
   him alone shall you adore" (Lk. 4:8).*

WHAT IS IDOLATRY?

Idolatry is giving to a creature the supreme honor due to God alone. Secularism is a kind of practical idolatry whereby man is considered the purpose and goal of all human activity.

The Lord, your God, shall you fear; him shall you serve... (Dt. 6:13).*

WHAT IS SACRILEGE?

Sacrilege is the abuse of a person, place, or thing consecrated to God and His service.

Determined to destroy us once and for all,
they burned down every shrine of God in the country
   (Ps. 74:8).*

IN WHAT OTHER WAYS CAN WE FAIL TO RENDER GOD THE HONOR DUE HIM?

We can fail to render God the honor due Him if we placed too much trust in many external practices, without internal devotion. This is superstition.

We would dishonor God if we attributed to creatures powers which belong to God alone, by believing in horoscopes, dreams, crystal gazing, charms and the like; by consulting spiritualists; by the use of magic; by satanism, which is invocation of the devil.

There must never be anyone among you who...uses charms, consults ghosts or spirits, or calls up the dead (Dt. 18:10-11).**

HOW DO WE WORSHIP GOD?

We worship God with public and private prayer, especially the Mass or Eucharistic Celebration—and with acts of faith, hope, and charity.

WHAT ARE THE MAIN REASONS FOR PRAYING?

The main reasons for praying are: To adore God; to thank Him; to ask His forgiveness and make up for sin; to ask His help for ourselves and others.

WHAT IS THE DIFFERENCE BETWEEN ADORATION AND VENERATION?

Adoration is the worship we give to God alone as the infinitely holy and Supreme Being. Veneration is the honor we give to the Blessed Virgin as the Mother of God, and to the angels and saints as the special friends of God.

HOW DOES THE CATHOLIC CHURCH HONOR MARY THE MOTHER OF GOD?

The Catholic Church honors the Mother of God with a special type of veneration in her liturgical and devotional prayers, and especially encourages the faithful to pray to, imitate, and love the Blessed Virgin.

WHY DOES THE CHURCH HONOR THE SAINTS?

The Church honors the saints (1) because they are the chosen friends of God; by honoring them, we honor God Himself; (2) because, by the example of their lives, they encourage us to grow in faith, hope, and love.

WHY DOES THE CHURCH HONOR THE ANGELS?

The Church honors the angels because they constantly adore the Trinity, and because they are God's special messengers to assist human beings on the path of salvation. (See also pages 31-34.)

IN VENERATING RELICS AND SACRED IMAGES, DO WE PRAY TO OR ADORE THEM?

We do not pray to or adore relics and sacred images, but we honor and pray to the persons whom they represent.

Prayer-Communication with God

HOW DO WE COMMUNICATE WITH GOD?

We communicate with God through prayer which is conversation with Him.

Sing joyfully to God our strength (Ps. 81:2).*

HOW MAY PRAYER BE DESCRIBED?

Prayer may be described as talking with God with mind and heart and often with voice as well. Jesus said:

"Come to me, all you who are weary and find life burdensome, and I will refresh you" (Mt. 11:28).*
(See also: Mt. 26:41; Jn. 4:21-24; 16:24; 1 Pt. 4:7.)

WHY DO WE PRAY?

We pray to praise and adore God. He is our Creator; we are His creatures. We pray to thank Him for all that He has done for us. We pray to ask pardon for our sins. We pray to ask the blessings and graces we need.

Be happy at all times; pray constantly; and for all things give thanks to God, because this is what God expects you to do in Christ Jesus (1 Thes. 5:17-18).**

WHAT KINDS OF PRAYERS ARE FOUND IN THE BIBLE?

—Prayers of praise:

"Holy, holy, holy, is the Lord God Almighty,
He who was, and who is, and who is to come!"
(Rv. 4:8)*

— Prayers of love for God:

As the hind longs for the running waters,
   so my soul longs for you, O God (Ps. 42:2).*

— Prayers of faith:

"You are the Messiah,...the Son of the living God!" (Mt. 16:16)*

— Prayers of sorrow:

"O God, be merciful to me, a sinner" (Lk. 18:13).*

— Prayers in time of need:

"Jesus, Son of David, have pity on me!" (Lk. 18:38)*

HOW OFTEN SHOULD WE PRAY?

We should pray often each day as St. Paul says:

...Never cease praying, render constant thanks; such is God's will for you in Christ Jesus (1 Thes. 5:17-18).*

And again:

Pray constantly and attentively (Eph. 6:18).*

WHAT IS THE MANNER IN WHICH WE SHOULD PRAY?

We should pray with faith, confident in the mercy and love of God; we should pray with humility, conscious of who God is and how "little" we are; we should pray with attention, fervor and perseverance.

"You should be awake, and praying not to be put to the test" (Mk. 14:38).**

FOR WHOM SHOULD WE PRAY?

We should pray for our own selves, for our immediate family, relatives, friends and neighbors, for the Pope, bishops, priests and religious, for government leaders, lawmakers, judges and public officials, for sinners, unbelievers, for the suffering souls in purgatory, and even for our enemies.

My advice is that, first of all, there should be prayers offered for everyone—petitions, intercessions and thanksgiving—and especially for kings and others in authority... (1 Tm. 2:1-2).**

IS EVERY PRAYER HEARD BY GOD?

Every prayer is heard by God and answered by Him according to the best designs of His holy will.

...If we ask him for anything,
and it is in accordance with his will,
he will hear us (1 Jn. 5:14).**

HOW DO WE KNOW THAT EVERY PRAYER IS HEARD BY GOD?

We know that every prayer is heard by God because Jesus has said:

"Ask, and it will be given to you; search, and you will find; knock, and the door will be opened to you. For the one who asks always receives; the one who searches always finds; the one who knocks will always have the door opened to him" (Mt. 7:7-8).**

(See also: Mt. 6:5-6, 6:25-27, 15:7-8, Lk. 18:9-14, Jn. 14:13, Jn. 15:7; Jn. 16:23-24, Heb. 4:16, Heb. 5:7, Jas. 1:5-6, Jas. 5:16, 1 Jn. 5:14-15.)

IF EVERY PRAYER IS ANSWERED, WHY DO WE NOT ALWAYS OBTAIN WHAT WE PRAY FOR?

We do not always obtain what we pray for in the manner in which we expected it either because we have not prayed properly or because God sees that what we are asking would not be for our good.

"You will receive all that you pray for, provided you have faith" (Mt. 21:22).*

WHY SHOULD GOD ANSWER OUR PRAYERS IN A MANNER OTHER THAN WHAT WE ARE ASKING?

God could answer our prayers in a manner other than what we are asking because He knows what is best for us. He knows what would be to our best advantage spiritually and even physically. With the Psalmist we can pray:

O God, be not far from me;
my God, make haste to help me (Ps. 71:12).*

WHY ARE WE SOMETIMES DISTRACTED WHEN WE PRAY?

We are sometimes distracted when we pray because of worry, anxiety or physical discomfort. Other distractions come from the devil. The effort made to overcome distractions makes our prayer very pleasing to God.

SHOULD WE PRAY IN TIME OF TROUBLE?

We *should* pray in time of trouble as St. James writes:

If anyone among you is suffering hardship, he must pray (Jas. 5:13).*

BASICALLY, HOW MANY KINDS OF PRAYER ARE THERE?

Basically, there are two kinds of prayer, vocal and mental prayer.

WHAT IS VOCAL PRAYER?

Vocal prayer is prayer of mind, heart and lips— prayer spoken audibly.

Lord, open my lips,
and my mouth will speak out your praise (Ps. 51:15).**

WHAT IS MENTAL PRAYER?

Mental prayer is unspoken prayer in which a person unites himself to God and ponders His truths.

WHAT IS MEDITATION?

Meditation is a kind of mental (unspoken) prayer in which a person, after quiet reflection, arrives at or strengthens a resolution to live a better Christian life.

Reflect on the injunctions of the Lord,
   busy yourself at all times with his commandments.
He will strengthen your mind,
   and the wisdom you desire will be granted you
(Sir. 6:37).**

WHAT ARE SOME OF THE VOCAL PRAYERS THAT EVERY CATHOLIC SHOULD KNOW BY HEART?

The vocal prayers that every Catholic should know by heart are the Our Father, Hail Mary, the Apostles' Creed, the Glory Be to the Father, Acts of Faith, Hope, Love and Contrition, the Morning Offering, Hail Holy Queen, Angel of God, grace before and after meals, Eternal Rest for the souls in purgatory.

WHY IS IT IMPORTANT TO PRAY AT TIMES WITH OTHERS?

It is important to pray at times with others because Jesus has said:

"Where two or three are gathered in my name, there am I in their midst" (Mt. 18:20).*

WHAT IS THE GREATEST COMMUNITY PRAYER?

The greatest community prayer is the Mass.

WHAT IS THE SIGN OF THE CROSS?

The Sign of the Cross is a special prayer which reminds us of two important mysteries of our faith: the Blessed Trinity and the Redemption.

WHEN DO WE USUALLY MAKE THE SIGN OF THE CROSS?

We usually make the Sign of the Cross when we begin and end our prayers.

HOW ARE THE MYSTERIES OF THE BLESSED TRINITY AND REDEMPTION EXPRESSED IN THE SIGN OF THE CROSS?

The mysteries of the Blessed Trinity and Redemption are expressed in this manner: when we say "In the name," we express the truth that there is just one God. When we say, "of the Father, and of the Son, and of the Holy Spirit," we manifest our belief that there are three distinct Persons in God. When we make the form of the cross on ourselves, we express our belief that the Son of God made man redeemed us by His death on the cross.

WHAT IS THE DIVINE OFFICE?

The Divine Office is the public and official common prayer of the Catholic Church. It is recited daily by priests and religious. The prayers are contained in the *Liturgy of the Hours.*

WHAT IS AN EJACULATION?

An ejaculation is a short prayer. It may also be known as an aspiration.

WHAT IS A NOVENA?

A *novena* is special prayers or devotions carried out for nine days in a row.

WHAT IS THE PURPOSE OF MAKING THE WAY (STATIONS) OF THE CROSS?

The purpose of making the Way of the Cross is to ponder the passion of Jesus and what He suffered for love of us. This practice can greatly increase our personal commitment to Jesus.

WHAT IS MEANT BY DEVOTION TO THE SACRED HEART?

By devotion to the Sacred Heart is meant that our Savior, Jesus, is especially honored because of His great love, by which He gave His life for us.

SECOND COMMANDMENT

WHAT IS THE SECOND COMMANDMENT OF GOD?

The second commandment of God is:

"You shall not take the name of the Lord, your God, in vain" (Ex. 20:7).*

WHAT DOES THE SECOND COMMANDMENT OBLIGE US TO DO?

The second commandment obliges us always to speak reverently of God, of the Blessed Virgin, of the angels and the saints.

Blessed be the name of the Lord
  both now and forever (Ps. 113:2).*

WHAT ELSE DOES THE SECOND COMMANDMENT REQUIRE OF US?

The second commandment also requires us to be truthful in taking oaths and faithful in fulfilling vows.

WHY SHOULD WE SPEAK RESPECTFULLY OF HOLY PERSONS, PLACES, AND THINGS?

We should speak respectfully of holy persons, places and things because they are consecrated to God.

MAY THE WORDS OF SACRED SCRIPTURE EVER BE USED IN A BAD OR WORLDLY SENSE?

The words of Sacred Scripture may never be used in a bad or worldly sense. Neither should they be ridiculed, used for jokes nor given any other meaning than what we believe God intended.

WHAT IS PROFANITY?

Profanity is the irreverent use of the name of God, Christ or the saints through impatience, jest, surprise or habit.

WHAT IS AN OATH?

An oath is a declaration before God that what we say is true.

Men, of course, swear an oath by something greater than themselves, and between men, confirmation by an oath puts an end to all dispute (Heb. 6:16).**

IS IT LAWFUL TO TAKE AN OATH?

It is lawful to take an oath because it is a guarantee of the truth.

WHAT CONDITIONS MAKE AN OATH LAWFUL?

The conditions which make an oath lawful are: 1) sufficient reason for taking an oath; 2) conviction that we speak the truth; 3) that the intention for taking the oath is not sinful.

> If you swear, "As Yahweh lives!"
> truthfully, justly, honestly,
> the nations will bless themselves by you,
> and glory in you (Jer. 4:2).**

WHEN MAY AN OATH BE TAKEN?

An oath may be taken when it concerns the glory of God, the good of our neighbor or our own personal good.

IS AN UNLAWFUL OATH OR VOW BINDING?

An unlawful oath or vow is not binding. Such oaths or vows are not to be taken and the fulfillment of them is sinful.

WHAT IS PERJURY?

Perjury is the calling upon God to bear witness to a lie. Perjury is also committed when, while under oath, one confirms with certainty something which is unknown or doubtful.

> You must not swear falsely by my name, profaning the name of your God (Lv. 19:12).**

WHAT IS BLASPHEMY?

Blasphemy is any word, thought or action which shows contempt for God, the Blessed Virgin, the angels, saints or religion.

> "Any man who curses his God shall bear the burden of his fault..." (Lv. 24:16).**

WHAT TWO CONDITIONS ARE NECESSARY FOR BLASPHEMY TO OCCUR?

Two conditions necessary for blasphemy to occur are: 1) knowledge of God and the sacred; 2) deliberate contempt for the same.

WHAT IS CURSING?

Cursing is the calling down of evil on some person, place or thing.

He loved cursing, may it recoil on him,
had no taste for blessing, may it shun him! (Ps. 109:17)**

IS THE CURSING OF ANIMALS OR INANIMATE OBJECTS SINFUL?

The cursing of animals or inanimate objects is sinful only because of the lack of virtue shown in uncontrolled anger or impatience.

IS CURSING A MAN WITH MORAL EVIL SINFUL?

To curse a man with moral evil is always sinful according to the degree of intent in wishing the spiritual evil.

IS CURSING A MAN WITH PHYSICAL EVIL ALWAYS SINFUL?

To curse a man with physical evil is always sinful unless the intention is for the man's own or another's spiritual well-being. To do so out of malice is always sinful and the seriousness depends on the evil intended.

WHAT IS A VOW?

A vow is a free and deliberate promise made to God by which a person binds himself under pain of sin to do something which is possible, morally good, and better than its voluntary omission.

"If you make a vow to Yahweh your God, you must not be lazy in keeping it;...the vow that you have freely made with your own mouth to Yahweh your God must be fulfilled" (Dt. 23:22, 24). (For vows that religious take, see pages 199-200.)

WHAT KIND OF VOWS ARE THERE?

There are two kinds of vows: public vows which are accepted in the name of the Church by a lawful religious superior, and private vows which are made directly to God by the individual.

WHAT ARE "PERSONAL" VOWS?

"Personal" vows are those concerning the actions the person will perform in order to fulfill the vow.

WHAT ARE "REAL" VOWS?

"Real" vows are those in which a physical object is promised to God.

WHICH VOWS ARE MADE MOST FREQUENTLY?

The vows made most frequently are those of poverty, chastity and obedience taken by persons living in religious communities or consecrated to God.

Sometimes persons living in the world are permitted to take such vows but they should do so only with the consent of their confessor.

IS THERE A DIFFERENCE BETWEEN MERE PROMISES AND VOWS?

Promises are made simply to oneself or to others, whereas a vow is a conscious and deliberate promise made to God.

WHAT SHOULD BE REMEMBERED BEFORE MAKING A VOW?

It should be remembered that the vow is made to God and therefore one is obliged to fulfill what he promised.

If you make a vow to God, discharge it without delay, for God has no love for fools (Eccl. 5:3).**

MAY WE DISREGARD THE FULFILLMENT OF OUR VOWS?

We may not disregard the fulfillment of our vows. To do so would be sinful, more or less grievously, according to the nature of the vow and the intention we had when we made it.

THIRD COMMANDMENT

WHAT IS THE THIRD COMMANDMENT?

The third commandment is:

"Remember the sabbath day and keep it holy" (Ex. 20:8).**
Worship the maker of heaven and earth and sea (Rv. 14:7).**

WHAT DOES THE THIRD COMMANDMENT TELL US TO AVOID?

The third commandment tells us to avoid all unnecessary servile work on Sundays and Holy Days of Obligation. What is said in this section about Sundays applies also to Holy Days of Obligation.

...The seventh day must be a day of complete rest, consecrated to Yahweh [God] (Ex. 31:15).**

WHAT IS SERVILE WORK?

Servile work is that which requires labor of body rather than labor of mind. To perform unnecessary servile work on Sunday for a notable time can be sinful.

WHY ARE WE COMMANDED TO REST FROM SERVILE WORK?

We are commanded to rest from servile work in order to direct our mind to heavenly things, to relax our body and refresh ourselves with wholesome recreation.

IS SERVILE WORK EVER LAWFUL ON SUNDAYS?

Servile work is lawful on Sundays if it is necessary and cannot be conveniently postponed, or if it is done for the honor of God (such as preparing the place for Mass) or the good of the community (such as the work of firemen, policemen, etc.).

WHAT ARE WE COMMANDED BY THE THIRD COMMANDMENT?

By the third commandment we are commanded to worship God on Sunday by participating in the holy Sacrifice of the Mass. A Saturday evening Mass may be attended to fulfill the obligation when permitted.

WHAT IS THE MASS?

The Mass is the sacrifice of Calvary made present on our altars so that we may share in the benefits of the Redemption; a memorial of the death and resurrection of Christ; a sacred banquet in which Christ is received. (See entire section on the Mass.)

WHAT IS THE BEST WAY OF PARTICIPATING IN THE HOLY SACRIFICE OF THE MASS?

The best way of participating in the holy Sacrifice is to offer it to God in union with the priest, uniting oneself interiorly and exteriorly with Christ the Victim, and by receiving Him in holy Communion.

HOW IS THE UNITY OF GOD'S PEOPLE EXPRESSED IN THE MASS?

The unity of God's people is expressed by the actions of the faithful who pray, sing and act together in the Mass. Most of all it is expressed in the receiving of the Holy Eucharist which is the center of unity.

WHY IS SUNDAY SET ASIDE AS A SPECIAL DAY?

Sunday is set aside as a special day because of a tradition handed down from the Apostles which took its origin from the very day of Christ's resurrection. This day bears the name of the Lord's day or Sunday.

Cf. Constitution on the Sacred Liturgy, no. 106

CAN WE NOT WORSHIP GOD IN OUR OWN HEARTS INSTEAD OF PARTICIPATING AT MASS?

No, interior worship is not enough. God created man with both body and soul. Hence, man must worship God with both, that is, interiorly and exteriorly. This worship also gives good example to others. Moreover, by participating at Mass with other believers we glorify God as social beings.

WHAT ACTIVITIES ARE ESPECIALLY SUITED TO MAKE SUNDAY A HOLY DAY?

Especially suited are activities which renew our soul and body, for example: reading a good book, doing works of charity, cultivating our cultural interests and wholesome recreation.

FOURTH COMMANDMENT

WHAT IS THE FOURTH COMMANDMENT?

The fourth commandment of God is:

Honor your father and your mother.... (Ex. 20:12)**

Children, obey your parents in the Lord, for that is what is expected of you. "Honor your father and mother" is the first commandment to carry a promise with it— "that it may go well with you and that you may have a long life on the earth" (Eph. 6:1-3).*

WHAT DOES THE FOURTH COMMANDMENT FORBID?

The fourth commandment forbids all disrespect, unkindness, stubbornness, spitefulness, complaints and disobedience toward our parents and lawful authorities.

WHAT DOES THE FOURTH COMMANDMENT OBLIGE US TO DO?

The fourth commandment orders us to love our parents, to respect and obey them in all that is not contrary to God's law and to help them in all their needs.

WHAT IS THE SOURCE AND BASIS OF PARENTAL AUTHORITY?

God Himself is the source of parental authority, and therefore children have a strict moral obligation to obey and care for their parents.

HOW DO CHILDREN SHOW THEIR LOVE AND RESPECT FOR THEIR PARENTS?

Children show their love and respect for their parents when they speak and act with gratitude, try to please them, readily accept corrections, seek advice in important decisions, patiently bear with their parents' faults, and pray for them.

> He who honors his father atones for sins;
>> he stores up riches who reveres his mother
>>> (Sir. 3:3-4).*

ARE WE OBLIGED TO RESPECT AND OBEY OTHERS BESIDES OUR PARENTS?

Besides our parents, the fourth commandment obliges us to respect and obey our teachers and lawful superiors, civil and ecclesiastical, when they discharge their official duties in conformity with the law of God.

You must all obey the governing authorities. Since all government comes from God, the civil authorities were appointed by God, and so anyone who resists authority is rebelling against God's decision... (Rom. 13:1-2).**

ARE CHILDREN OBLIGED TO OBEY THEIR PARENTS ABOUT THEIR CHOICE AS TO A STATE IN LIFE?

Children should ordinarily ask their parents' advice about their choice as to a state in life, but they are not always obliged to follow their parents' advice. Parents must not force their children in their choice of a state in life nor prevent them from fulfilling it.

WHAT ARE THE DUTIES OF PARENTS TOWARD THEIR CHILDREN?

Parents must love their children, have their children baptized as soon as possible, provide for their material welfare, instruct them and give them a Christian education, correct their defects, train them by word and example in the practice of Christian virtue, and counsel and guide them in forming a correct moral conscience.

The man who fails to use the stick hates his son;
the man who is free with his correction loves him
(Prv. 13:24).** (See also Sir. 7:23; Eph. 6:4.)

HOW CAN PARENTS FULFILL THEIR RESPONSIBILITY OF KEEPING STRONG THE FAMILY BONDS OF UNION?

Parents can fulfill their special responsibility of keeping the family strongly united by family prayer, family sacrifice and family liturgy.

WHAT ARE SOME DUTIES OF WORKMEN TOWARD THEIR EMPLOYERS?

Some duties of workmen toward their employers are to serve them faithfully and honestly and to guard against injury to the property and good name of their employer.

WHAT ARE SOME DUTIES OF EMPLOYERS TO THEIR WORKERS?

Employers must see to it that their workers are fairly and justly treated and that their wages are justly payed.

ARE WE OBLIGED TO OBEY CIVIL LAWS WHEN THEY ARE CONTRARY TO GOD'S LAW?

If the civil law obliges citizens to violate the law of God, they must refuse to obey, for it is "Better for us to obey God than men!" (Acts 5:29)*

WHAT ARE THE DUTIES OF A CITIZEN TOWARD HIS COUNTRY?

The principal duties of a citizen toward his country are: to respect civil authority, and obey just laws; that is, conscientiously fulfill all civil duties.

"Give back to Caesar what belongs to Caesar—and to God what belongs to God" (Lk. 20:25).**

WHAT ARE THE PRINCIPAL CIVIL DUTIES?

The principal civil duties are: to pay taxes; to defend one's country, even at the cost of one's life; to fulfill one's duty of voting; to work for and support laws which protect Christian morals and the common good.

IS THE OBLIGATION OF BEARING ARMS IN THE SERVICE OF ONE'S COUNTRY BINDING UPON ALL?

The obligation to serve one's country allows for those who, for reasons of conscience, refuse to bear arms, provided however that they agree to serve the community in some other way.

WHAT ARE THE DUTIES OF CATHOLICS WITH REGARD TO VOTING?

Catholics must vote for people whose beliefs and programs are sincerely beneficial to everyone.

IS IT A SIN TO VOTE FOR AN ENEMY OF RELIGION?

It is a sin to vote for an enemy of religion or of the national well-being because, by voting for him, one voluntarily participates in the evil which such a person could do if he were elected.

IS IT A SIN NOT TO VOTE?

It could be a sin not to vote, if, by not voting, one were the cause of an incompetent or perverse candidate being elected.

FIFTH COMMANDMENT

WHAT IS THE FIFTH COMMANDMENT OF GOD?
The fifth commandment of God is

"You shall not kill" (Ex. 20:13).*
In his hand is the soul of every living thing,
and the life breath of all mankind (Job 12:10).*

WHAT DOES THE FIFTH COMMANDMENT COMMAND?
The fifth commandment commands us to take proper care of our own life and the lives of others. We may also treat here some attacks on the life of the soul.

WHAT ARE SOME OF THE CHIEF CRIMES COMMITTED AGAINST HUMAN LIFE AND DIGNITY?
Some of the chief crimes committed against human life and dignity are any type of murder such as abortion, euthanasia or "mercy-killing," suicide; mutilation and/or sterilization of the human body without a serious reason, torture and brainwashing, indecent living and working conditions, forced imprisonment of innocent people, being deported from one's country, slavery, and the selling of women and children.

DOES THE FIFTH COMMANDMENT "YOU SHALL NOT KILL" APPLY TO ALL INNOCENT HUMAN LIFE?
Yes, the commandment, "You shall not kill" applies to all innocent human life, including that of the unborn child, who has the same right to life as any other human person. Abortion at any time after the child is conceived in the womb of his mother deprives the unborn of this basic right, and therefore is murder.

IS IT EVER PERMISSIBLE TO KNOWINGLY SHORTEN ONE'S LIFE?

It is sinful to directly intend to shorten one's life, e.g., by choosing to work under dangerous conditions in the hope of shortening one's own life. But a person may risk his life or health for a serious motive, e.g., to save the life of another person.

IS EUTHANASIA OR "MERCY-KILLING" AGAINST THE FIFTH COMMANDMENT?

Euthanasia, or "mercy-killing," is always a grave sin because no human person has the right over his own life or that of another. God alone is the Lord and Master of life. The sin committed is either suicide or murder.

IS DRUG ABUSE SINFUL?

Drug abuse is sinful because it can seriously injure our mental and/or physical well-being. Drugs also make it easy for us to do wrong to ourselves or to others.

IS MUTILATION OF THE HUMAN BODY EVER PERMITTED?

Mutilation of the human body—for example: removing an arm, leg, etc.—may be permitted if there is no other way to preserve the health or save the life of a person.

WHAT DOES THE CHURCH TEACH CONCERNING STERILIZATION?

If sterilization is performed to take away a man's or woman's power to reproduce offspring for one's own satisfaction, or economic or social needs, such actions are grievously wrong. If sterilization is necessary because of serious health reasons, then no sin is involved.

WHEN MAY IT BE LAWFUL TO TAKE THE LIFE OF ANOTHER PERSON?

It may be lawful to take the life of another person, 1) to protect one's own life and possessions and those of one's neighbor from an unjust attacker, provided no other means of protection is effective; 2) in fighting a just war; 3) to execute just punishment for a crime, though many Catholic thinkers hold that capital punishment is not justified in our time.

IN WHAT MANNER ARE WE OBLIGED TO TAKE CARE OF OUR PHYSICAL HEALTH?

We are obliged to use ordinary means (food, sleep, shelter, medical attention) to preserve our life. Extraordinary means, i.e., those which involve very great pain, expense, or other extreme difficulties, may not be obligatory. Church authorities may be consulted when there is doubt.

WHY MUST WE ALSO TAKE CARE OF OUR SPIRITUAL WELL-BEING AND THAT OF OUR NEIGHBOR?

Our spiritual well-being is even more important than our physical well-being, because we are not destined for this life alone but for eternal life.

IN WHAT OTHER WAYS DO WE FAIL AGAINST THE FIFTH COMMANDMENT?

We fail against the fifth commandment by quarreling, fighting, anger, hatred, revenge, drunkenness, and the taking of harmful or dangerous drugs.

WHAT DID CHRIST TEACH US ABOUT LOVE AND FORGIVENESS?

Christ taught us to pray in the "Our Father":

Forgive us our trespasses, as we forgive those who trespass against us.

He Himself has given us the supreme example: from the cross He prayed for all those responsible for His death:

"Father, forgive them; they do not know what they are doing" (Lk. 23:34).

Anger, hatred, fighting, etc., are directly opposed to Christ's great law of love:

"Love your neighbor as yourself" (Mt. 22:39).**

He added:

"Love your enemies and pray for those who persecute you..." (Mt. 5:44).**

IN WHAT OTHER WAY DO WE RESPECT THE SPIRITUAL WELL-BEING OF OTHERS?

We respect the spiritual well-being of others by always giving good example in our private and public life.

To give scandal or serious bad example by leading another to sin by word, action, or omission, or by lessening his respect for God and religion, can be sinful.

WHAT ARE SOME SOURCES OF SCANDAL?

Some sources of scandal or bad example are neglect of the practice of one's religion; use of improper or bad language; immoral films, TV and radio programs, and literature; immodest styles; and the example of bad companions.

WHAT RESPONSIBILITY DO THOSE HAVE WHO TAKE PART IN THE PRODUCTION OR TRANSMISSION OF MASS MEDIA PRESENTATIONS?

Those who have the responsibility for mass media must be acquainted with the norms of morality and conscientiously put them into practice in this area.

WHAT OBLIGATION DO READERS, LISTENERS, AND VIEWERS HAVE WITH REGARD TO USE OF THE MEDIA?

Readers, listeners and viewers are obliged to choose only what is morally good and honestly truthful. They must avoid whatever can be a cause of spiritual harm for themselves or others. In addition, parents have a duty to guard their children from any morally harmful influence from the media, and to form themselves and their children to use the media with an upright conscience.

ARE WE TO RESPECT ALL PEOPLE?

Yes, we are to respect all people because all people, created in the image and likeness of God, have been redeemed by Christ and are destined for eternal life. Therefore, every type of prejudice is to be overcome and rooted out as contrary to God's intent and to human dignity.

...This is the commandment which you have heard since the beginning, to live a life of love (2 Jn. 6).**

WHEN IS A WAR JUST?

For a war to be just, 1) it must be called for by the head of the government, 2) those who are undertaking war should have a rightful intention, 3) there must be a just cause, 4) other means of settlement must have been tried and failed, 5) the evils of conflict must not outweigh the good results to be expected from waging war.... Applying those principles is very difficult today.

HOW CAN CHRISTIANS CONTRIBUTE TO THE ESTABLISHMENT OF TRUE PEACE?

Christians can contribute to the establishment of true peace first, by rooting out all causes of discord (injustice, distrust, pride, envy, and other selfish passions) in their own lives.

Second, by offering financial, professional, and moral support to national and international institutes whose aim is to aid developing nations and work for cooperation among nations.

SIXTH AND NINTH COMMANDMENTS

WHAT IS THE SIXTH COMMANDMENT OF GOD?
The sixth commandment of God is this:
"You shall not commit adultery" (Ex. 20:14).*

WHAT IS THE NINTH COMMANDMENT OF GOD?
The ninth commandment of God is this:
"You shall not covet your neighbor's wife" (Ex. 20:17).**

WHAT DO THE SIXTH AND NINTH COMMAND-MENTS OBLIGE US TO DO?
The sixth commandment obliges us to be pure and modest in behavior both when alone and with others.
The ninth commandment obliges us to be pure in thoughts and desires.

WHY ARE THESE TWO COMMANDMENTS STUDIED TOGETHER?
We study the sixth and ninth commandments together because both concern the virtue of purity: external purity (how we speak and act) in the sixth commandment, and internal purity (how we think, imagine, and desire) in the ninth commandment.

WHAT IS PURITY?
Purity, or chastity, is that virtue by which we properly regulate our use of the sexual acts according to our state in life.

WHAT IS MODESTY?

Modesty is that virtue which inclines us to guard our senses so as to avoid possible temptations. It also causes us to refrain from whatever might incite others to sin and to be proper in dress and behavior.

WHAT SINS ARE FORBIDDEN BY THE SIXTH AND NINTH COMMANDMENTS?

The sixth commandment of God forbids impure acts, that is, the illegitimate pleasures of sex, and everything that leads to impurity.

The ninth commandment forbids impure thoughts sought or entertained with pleasure: impure imaginings voluntarily excited or not rejected, and evil desires.

ARE ALL UNCHASTE TEMPTATIONS SINFUL?

Temptations against the sixth and ninth commandments are not sinful in themselves, but we must reject impure thoughts at once, ignore them or try to distract ourselves by other thoughts and by prayer. They only become sinful when the thought of the unchaste action, an unchaste desire or passion is deliberately aroused and is willingly consented to or indulged in.

WHAT ARE THE MAIN SINS COMMITTED AGAINST THESE TWO COMMANDMENTS?

The main sins committed against these two commandments are: adultery, unreasonable denial of marital rights, fornication (sex between a man and woman who are not husband and wife), abortion, contraception, homosexuality, prostitution, pre-marital sex, self-abuse (masturbation), deliberate thoughts, words or actions which arouse unlawful sexual feelings, reading obscene literature, watching immoral movies, TV, plays, shows, indecent photographs or paintings, listening to or dancing to suggestive music.

CAN WE NOT ACT IN THESE MATTERS BY OUR OWN CONSCIENCE?

We must certainly judge all of our actions by our own conscience, but first of all our conscience must be educated according to objective moral truth, that is, by the moral law given to us by our Creator. This requires that we know better the Scriptures and Church teachings, that we pray more.

"He who obeys the commandments he has from me is the man who loves me;
and he who loves me will be loved by my Father.
I too will love him
and reveal myself to him" (Jn. 14:21).*

HOW DO WE KNOW THE CHURCH IS RIGHT IN ITS JUDGMENT ON THESE MATTERS?

We know the Church judges rightly on these matters because she has the divine mandate from Christ to guard and interpret His morals. She is always aided by the Holy Spirit. Also we know that the Christian moral law is based on natural law.

"Do not imagine that I have come to abolish the Law or the Prophets. I have come not to abolish but to complete them. I tell you solemnly, till heaven and earth disappear, not one dot, not one little stroke, shall disappear from the Law until its purpose is achieved" (Mt. 5:17-18).**

IF ALL THESE RESTRICTIONS ARE PART OF THE NATURAL LAW, WHY DO WE FEEL SO INCLINED TOWARDS BREAKING THEM?

All these restrictions are part of the natural law because in each man's conscience is a built-in moral code. However, we feel inclined toward breaking them because original sin has weakened our nature, inclining us to these sins.

"The spirit is willing, but the flesh is weak" (Mk. 14:38).

The devil tempts us also. (See: Rev. 12:9; 1 Pt. 5:8-9; Wis. 2:24.)

WHY IS ADULTERY SERIOUSLY FORBIDDEN IN TWO WAYS?

Adultery is seriously forbidden in two ways because in breaking the union of marriage by using his sexual powers outside of that union, a person offends the virtue of chastity; and because by taking away the exclusive rights of another, (his or her partner in marriage), a person offends also the virtue of justice.

WHY ARE HOMOSEXUALITY AND MASTURBATION CONDEMNED BY THE CHURCH?

Homosexuality and masturbation are gravely forbidden because they violate "laws inscribed in the very being of man and of woman" (Humanae Vitae, 11, 12) and because they mock the divine plan:

...Male and female he created them.

God blessed them, saying to them, "Be fruitful, multiply, fill the earth and conquer it" (Gn. 1:27-28).**

WHAT DOES THE CHURCH TEACH CONCERNING ABORTION AND INFANTICIDE?

The Church teaches that abortion and infanticide (the killing of babies and children) are murder.

Truly you have formed my inmost being;
  you knit me in my mother's womb.
I give you thanks that I am fearfully, wonderfully made;
  wonderful are your works... (Ps. 139:13-14).

WHAT IS THE CHURCH'S TEACHING ON BIRTH CONTROL?

The Church condemns all forms of birth control such as pills, drugs, or mechanical devices, because these are against the natural purpose of married love, that is, the transmission or giving of life. If serious reasons warrant the limitation of births, Catholics may practice natural family planning. Couples may consult a priest or Catholic Natural Family Planning groups.

WHY MUST WE TREAT OUR BODY AS A SACRED THING?

We must treat our body as a sacred thing because it truly is, due to the fact that God lives within us by grace. St. Paul says:

Your body, you know, is the temple of the Holy Spirit, who is in you since you received him from God (1 Cor. 6:19).**

WHAT ARE THE PRINCIPAL MEANS FOR PRACTIC- ING PURITY?

The principal means for practicing this virtue are frequent Holy Communion and a great devotion to the Blessed Virgin.

In order to preserve oneself from impurity, one must also watch his actions, conversations, etc., and avoid, as much as possible, all dangerous occasions.

WHAT DANGERS ARE THERE EVER PRESENT AGAINST THE VIRTUE OF CHASTITY?

The ever-present dangers to chastity are:

1. idleness, which leads one into temptation;

2. bad company, which influences evil actions;

3. unbridled curiosity, which will find its way into dangerous occasions;

4. excessive eating and drinking, which lead man to seek continual bodily satisfaction;

5. immodest dress, which makes one a slave to appearance and attention, and which can be a grave temptation to others;

6. indecent, immoral reading, TV, movies, plays, shows, amusements and photographs, which implant strong, recurring impressions in the mind, etc.;

7. suggestive music, which by its rhythm or lyrics excites the sensual appetites;

8. obscene talk, which, besides causing temptation and scandal to others, gradually eats away man's moral sense.

SEVENTH
AND TENTH COMMANDMENTS

WHAT IS THE SEVENTH COMMANDMENT?
The seventh commandment is:
"You shall not steal" (Ex. 20:15).*

WHAT IS THE TENTH COMMANDMENT?
The tenth commandment is: You shall not covet your neighbor's goods.
"You shall not covet your neighbor's house...nor his male or female slave, nor his ox or ass, nor anything else that belongs to him" (Ex. 20:17).*

WHAT DUTY IS IMPOSED ON US BY THE SEVENTH AND TENTH COMMANDMENTS?
By these commandments we are obliged to be honest and to respect all that concerns the possessions of others.

WHAT DOES THE SEVENTH COMMANDMENT FORBID?
The seventh commandment forbids stealing and robbery, unjust acquisition of goods and reckless destruction of what belongs to others.

Stealing can be mortally sinful if the thing stolen is of considerable value (otherwise it is a venial sin).

Stealing something of small value can be mortally sinful if the owner is poor, and thus suffers great injury.

WHAT DOES THE TENTH COMMANDMENT FORBID?

The tenth commandment forbids even the desire to take or to keep our neighbor's goods.

ARE WE BOUND TO RETURN STOLEN GOODS?

We are bound to return stolen goods or their value in money to the owner or, if the owner is dead, to his family.

If neither the owner nor the family of the owner can be discovered, the goods or their value are to be given to the poor or to charitable causes.

WHAT ARE SOME MORE SUBTLE FORMS OF STEALING?

Some more subtle forms of stealing are: cheating the consumer as to the exact use of a machine or object being sold; hiding a defect in that object; doing poor work and repairs (through negligence); repairing machinery and changing parts unnecessarily; charging a price that deserves a better job; in politics, acquiring money or positions by dishonest means; making false insurance claims, etc.

WHAT IS A BRIBE?

A bribe is an offering of money or other valuable objects with the intention to corrupt. Bribery, obviously, is wrong and can be seriously wrong.

DOES MAN HAVE A RIGHT TO PRIVATE OWNERSHIP?

Yes, man has a right to private ownership. This right, bestowed on him by the Creator, provides man with the means for his livelihood, for his growth and progress.

CAN THIS PRINCIPLE OF PRIVATE OWNERSHIP JUSTIFY THE OVERABUNDANCE OF SOME AND THE EXTREME POVERTY OF OTHERS?

The principle of private ownership does not justify the overabundance of some and the extreme poverty of others. No one is justified in keeping for his exclusive use what he does not need, when others lack necessities.

WHAT SHOULD BE THE EMPLOYER'S ATTITUDE?

The employer's attitude should be one of equity (or fairness) — justice with charity, thus assuring his workers just wages, proper and dignified working conditions and reasonable safety on the job.

WHEN ARE WORKERS PERMITTED TO STRIKE?

Workers are permitted to strike when their rights are violated, lawful contracts ignored or other serious difficulties arise.

The strike, however, can be used only after all the other means to solve the difficulties have produced negative results.

Moreover, a strike must be conducted in a fair and peaceful manner, avoiding all forms of violence.

WHAT ARE SOME OF THE WORKERS' DUTIES?

Workers have the duty to produce good work, to take reasonable care of the employer's property, to avoid damaging working materials through carelessness, to occupy well the working hours.

IS ONE OBLIGED TO MAKE UP FOR DAMAGE DONE?

One is obliged to make up for damage unjustly done to the property of others, as far as one is able.

WHAT IS GAMBLING?

Gambling is the staking of money or valuables on a future event or on a game of chance, the result of which is unknown to the participants.

IS IT WRONG TO GAMBLE?

Gambling in itself can be an amusement, and it is not against Catholic moral standards if played fairly and honestly and with moderation.

However, gambling can become a sin, even a mortal sin, if it leads one to excesses such as dishonesty, and great loss of money, risking the needs of the family and even of society.

EIGHTH COMMANDMENT

WHAT IS THE EIGHTH COMMANDMENT?

The eighth commandment of God is:

"You shall not bear false witness against your neighbor" (Ex. 20:16).

...From now on, there must be no more lies: *You must speak the truth to one another,* since we are all parts of one another (Eph. 4:25).**

WHAT DUTY IS IMPOSED ON US BY THE EIGHTH COMMANDMENT?

By the eighth commandment we are obliged to be truthful and to interpret in the best possible way the actions of others.

WHAT MUST BE AVOIDED BY THE EIGHTH COMMANDMENT?

By the eighth commandment we must avoid rash judgments, suspicions, detraction (taking away the good name of another), lying and calumny (telling the hidden faults of another), talebearing and the telling of secrets we are bound to keep.

WHAT IS A LIE?

A lie is something said usually for the purpose of deceiving others, which we know or suspect to be untrue.

The false witness will not go unpunished,
the man who utters lies will meet his end (Prv. 19:9).**

WILL A GOOD REASON FOR TELLING A LIE EXCUSE IT?

No reason, however good, will excuse the telling of a lie, because a lie is always bad in itself: It is never allowed, even for a good intention, to do a thing that is bad in itself.

WHAT IS A JOCOSE LIE?

A jocose lie is a story made up for the purpose of amusing or instructing others. It becomes sinful if the person telling it does not make it clear that it must not be taken literally.

WHAT IS A MENTAL RESERVATION?

A mental reservation, made in circumstances when one is bound in conscience not to tell the entire truth, limits the sense of the speaker's words to a certain meaning.

WHAT IS THE DIFFERENCE BETWEEN STRICT AND BROAD MENTAL RESERVATION?

Strict mental reservation, which is really a lie, limits the meaning so much that there is only one way the statement could be taken and it is in a false way. It is never permitted.

Broad mental reservation, instead, gives a clue to the real meaning of the statement, and the truth can be known from it. It is permitted for sufficient reason.

WHAT IS RASH JUDGMENT?

Rash judgment is believing, without sufficient reason, something harmful to another's character.

WHY SHOULD MAKING RASH JUDGMENTS BE AVOIDED?

Every person has the right to be respected by other persons. When a rash judgment is made, it causes one to think less good of another person and this is opposed to charity.

WHAT IS DETRACTION?

Detraction is making known, without good reason, the hidden faults of others.

IS IT EVER ALLOWED TO TELL THE FAULTS OF ANOTHER?

It is allowed to tell the faults of another when it is necessary to make them known to his parents or superiors, that the faults may be corrected and the wrongdoer prevented from greater sin. If a person is convicted as a criminal, making known his faults is not detraction, because the person no longer has esteem in this matter. However, it is more charitable not to speak of them.

WHEN DOES SLANDER OR CALUMNY OCCUR?

Slander or calumny occurs when a person injures the good name of another by lying.

WHAT IS TALEBEARING?

Talebearing is the act of telling persons what others have said about them, especially if the things said are evil. It is wrong, because it gives rise to anger, hatred and ill-will, and is often the cause of greater sins.

WHEN ARE WE OBLIGED TO KEEP A SECRET?

We are obliged to keep a secret when we have promised to do so, when our office requires it, or when the good of others demands it.

WHAT IS A NATURAL SECRET?

A natural secret is one which natural law or right reason tells us should be kept.

WHAT IS A PROMISED SECRET?

A promised secret is one in which the information is made known and then the promise to conceal it is secured.

WHAT IS AN ENTRUSTED SECRET?

An entrusted secret is one in which the promise is made first and then the information is disclosed.

IS IT EVER PERMITTED TO READ OTHERS' LETTERS OR PRIVATE WRITINGS?

These may never be read without permission (even reasonably presumed) from the owner, unless the motive is to prevent grave harm to oneself, to another person or to society.

WHAT MUST A PERSON DO WHEN HE HAS SINNED BY DETRACTION OR CALUMNY?

The person must intend to repair the harm done to his neighbor, as far as is possible.

WHY DOES THE INDIVIDUAL AND SOCIETY AS A WHOLE HAVE A RIGHT TO INFORMATION?

Society needs information in order to make right decisions, and well-informed citizens contribute to their personal progress as well as the common good.

WHAT OTHER RIGHTS PARALLEL THE RIGHT TO INFORMATION?

The right to privacy for individuals, families and societies must be insured, as well as the right of secrecy, binding in conscience, for necessary or professional reasons.

WHAT IS THE DUTY OF THOSE WHO CONTROL THE MEDIA IN PRESENTING THE NEWS AND OTHER INFORMATION TO THE PUBLIC?

Those who control the media must always give what is true and as far as justice and charity permit, what is complete. This must be done with balanced judgment and prudence, so that not only the sensational is given, but what is of real importance.

WHAT IS THE DUTY OF LISTENERS AND VIEWERS REGARDING THE MEDIA?

Listeners and viewers have the duty to accept the truth, and to reject what is opposed to it. They do this by reacting to what is being presented to them. They should show dissatisfaction with distortions, omissions, biased reporting and the reporting of events out of context. They should also expect that mistakes made be corrected and that events should not be underplayed or exaggerated.

HOW IS PUBLIC OPINION JUSTLY PROMOTED?

The spreading of information that is, most importantly, of service to the truth and that recognizes human dignity and is for the benefit of all is the sure and just way to form public opinion.

WHAT IS THE RELATIONSHIP BETWEEN EDUCATION AND THE MEDIA?

The media, an excellent means of reaching the greatest number of people in the most effective way, should be used to educate humanity. Its presentations should encourage people to reflect upon what they see and to share their experiences with others, all for the common good.

WHAT IS TO BE SAID OF TRUTH IN ADVERTISING?

Truth in advertising means that making known various products and services to the advantage of men and society is a good thing, provided the freedom of choice of the individual is respected and the truth is not distorted or hidden.

Some Special Duties of Catholic Christians

Laws of the Church

DOES THE CATHOLIC CHURCH HAVE THE RIGHT TO MAKE LAWS?

The Catholic Church does have the right to make laws from its Founder, Jesus Christ, who said to the Apostles, His first leaders and bishops:

"Whatever you bind on earth shall be considered bound in heaven" (Mt. 16:19).** (See also: Lk. 10:16.)

BY WHOM IS THE CHURCH'S RIGHT TO MAKE LAWS EXERCISED?

The Church's right to make laws is exercised by the Pope and bishops united with him.

WHO HAS COMPLETE, SUPREME, ORDINARY AND IMMEDIATE JURISDICTION OVER THE UNIVERSAL CHURCH?

The Pope has complete, supreme, ordinary and immediate jurisdiction over the universal Church.
(See also the entire section on the Church.)

WHEN ELSE MAY LAWS BE MADE WHICH AFFECT THE UNIVERSAL CHURCH?

Laws which affect the universal Church may be made by a general council of bishops united with the Pope (for example: Vatican Council II).

WHAT IS MEANT BY PRECEPTS OF THE CHURCH?

The precepts of the Church are special duties which we, as Catholics, are expected to obey and fulfill.

WHICH ARE THE SPECIAL DUTIES OF CATHOLICS, CALLED THE PRECEPTS OF THE CHURCH?

Some duties expected of Catholics today include the following. (Those traditionally mentioned as Precepts of the Church or Laws of the Church are marked with an asterisk.)

1. To keep holy the day of the Lord's Resurrection: to worship God by participating in Mass every Sunday and Holy Day of Obligation:* to avoid those activities that would hinder renewal of soul and body, e.g., needless work and business activities, unnecessary shopping, etc.

2. To lead a sacramental life: to receive Holy Communion frequently and the sacrament of Penance regularly—
—minimally, to receive the sacrament of Penance at least once a year (annual confession is obligatory only if serious sin is involved).*
—minimally, to receive Holy Communion at least once a year, between the First Sunday of Lent and Trinity Sunday.*

3. To study Catholic teaching in preparation for the sacrament of Confirmation, to be confirmed, and then to continue to study and advance the cause of Christ.

4. To observe the marriage laws of the Church:* to give religious training (by example and word) to one's children; to use parish schools and religious education programs.

5. To strengthen and support the Church*: one's own parish community and parish priests; the worldwide Church and the Holy Father.

6. To do penance, including abstaining from meat and fasting from food on the appointed days.*

7. To join in the missionary spirit and apostolate of the Church (*Basic Teachings,* U.S. Bishops).

WHAT ARE THE HOLY DAYS OF OBLIGATION IN THE UNITED STATES?

The holy days of obligation in the United States are: —all the Sundays of the year

—January 1, the Solemnity of Mary, Mother of God

—Ascension of our Lord (forty days after Easter)

—August 15, the Assumption of the Blessed Virgin Mary

—November 1, All Saints' Day

—December 8, the Immaculate Conception

—December 25, Christmas Day.

IF A CATHOLIC, THROUGH NEGLIGENCE, MISSES MASS ON A SUNDAY (OR SATURDAY EVENING) OR HOLY DAY OF OBLIGATION, IS THERE SIN INVOLVED?

The Catholic who, through negligence, misses Mass on a Sunday (or Saturday evening) or holy day of obligation can commit a mortal sin.

IS IT SPIRITUALLY WISE TO EASILY EXEMPT OURSELVES FROM SUNDAY MASS?

It is not spiritually wise to easily exempt ourselves from Sunday Mass. The graces that we need to live fervent Catholic lives come to us through the Mass.

WHO ARE EXEMPT FROM ASSISTING AT SUNDAY OR HOLY DAY MASS?

Some of those exempted from assisting at Sunday or holy day Mass are:

— the sick and those who must care for them

— those who live a great distance from a Catholic Church

— those who have an urgent work (policeman, fireman, nurse on duty, etc.)

— those hampered by temporary difficulties such as weather (an elderly person in a snowstorm, or in very cold weather).

Anyone may freely consult a priest about his or her particular situation, and is encouraged to do so.

WHY HAS THE CHURCH INSTITUTED HOLY DAYS?

The Church has instituted holy days to recall to our minds the sacred mysteries of our Catholic Faith, and the important events in the lives of Jesus, Mary and the saints.

WHAT IS A FAST DAY?

A fast day is a day in which only one full meal is taken. The other two meals should not together equal a full meal.

WHY HAS THE CHURCH INSTITUTED FAST DAYS?

The Church has instituted fast days so that we Christians may learn to set our sights on God, and the destiny and goal of our life here on earth by denying our body. This is to follow the example of Jesus who

...was led into the desert by the Spirit to be tempted by the devil. He fasted forty days and forty nights, and afterward was hungry (Mt. 4:1-2).* (See also: Tob. 12:8, Joel 2:12, Mt. 6:16-18.)

WHO ARE OBLIGED TO FAST?

Catholics are obliged to fast who are between the ages of 21 and 59.

WHAT DOES THE LAW OF ABSTINENCE MEAN?

The law of abstinence means refraining from eating meat, and soups and gravies made from meat, on certain "days of abstinence" stipulated by the Church, such as Ash Wednesday.

WHICH ARE THE DAYS FOR ABSTINENCE FROM MEAT IN THE UNITED STATES?

The days for abstinence from meat in the United States are Ash Wednesday, the Fridays of Lent, and Good Friday. Catholics over 14 years of age are obliged to keep this law.

ARE FASTING AND ABSTINENCE THE ONLY "PENANCES" REQUIRED OF CATHOLICS?

Fasting and abstinence are not the only "penances" required by Catholics. We are to do more penances of our own choosing especially on Fridays throughout the year, since Jesus gave His life for us on a Friday, and during Lent, when we recall what the Lord suffered for us.

Christian Living and the People of God

WHAT IS A CHRISTIAN?

A Christian is a baptized follower of Jesus Christ. St. Paul said:

Imitate me as I imitate Christ (1 Cor. 11:1).*

WHAT IS CHRISTIAN MORALITY?

Christian morality is living in a way worthy of our dignity as human beings and God's adopted children.

...Be holy in all you do, since it is the Holy One who has called you, and scripture says: "Be holy, for I am holy" (1 Pt. 1:15-16).**

WHAT IS THE GREAT COMMANDMENT WHICH MUST BE LIVED BY ALL WHO BELIEVE IN GOD?

The Great Commandment which must be lived by all who believe in God is:

"You must love the Lord your God with all your heart, with all your soul, and with all your mind.... You must love your neighbor as yourself" (Mt. 22:37, 39).**

WHAT DOES JESUS' COMMANDMENT OF LOVE MEAN FOR US?

We are to love God with our whole being. We are to love others as Jesus loves us, and because God loves them and wants us to do the same. (See: Dt. 6:4f.)

TOWARDS WHOM DO WE HAVE DUTIES?

We have duties towards God, self and neighbor as our study of the Ten Commandments has shown us.

WHAT IS EVANGELIZATION?

Evangelization is the spreading of the Gospel—the Good News about what Jesus has done for us, what He expects of us, and what He promises us. Jesus says to us:

"I am the light of the world" (Jn. 8:12).**

"You are the light of the world" (Mt. 5:14).**

He also said:

"Go out to the whole world; proclaim the Good News to all creation" (Mk. 16:15).** (See also: Mt. 28:19-20.)

WHY DID JESUS CALL US THE "LIGHT OF THE WORLD"?

Jesus called us the "light of the world" because He wants us to lead good lives, and give the truth to others. St. Peter said:

...Go on growing in the grace and in the knowledge of our Lord and savior Jesus Christ (2 Pt. 3:18).**

WHICH ARE THE SPIRITUAL WORKS OF MERCY?

The spiritual works of mercy are: to counsel the doubtful, to instruct the ignorant, to admonish the sinner, to comfort the sorrowful, to forgive injuries, to bear wrongs patiently, to pray for the living and the dead.

WHICH ARE THE CORPORAL WORKS OF MERCY?

The corporal works of mercy are: to feed the hungry, to give drink to the thirsty, to clothe the naked, to shelter the homeless, to visit the sick, to visit the imprisoned, to bury the dead.

WHAT ARE THE EIGHT BEATITUDES?

The eight beatitudes are:

"How blest are the poor in spirit: the reign of God is theirs.

Blest too are the sorrowing; they shall be consoled.

[Blest are the lowly; they shall inherit the land.]

Blest are they who hunger and thirst for holiness; they shall have their fill.

Blest are they who show mercy; mercy shall be theirs.

Blest are the single-hearted for they shall see God.

Blest too the peacemakers; they shall be called sons of God.

Blest are those persecuted for holiness' sake; the reign of God is theirs.

Blest are you when they insult you and persecute you and utter every kind of slander against you because of me.

Be glad and rejoice, for your reward is great in heaven; they persecuted the prophets before you in the very same way" (Mt. 5:3-12).*

HOW DOES THE CATHOLIC LOOK UPON "SUFFERING" FOR THE FAITH?

The Catholic looks upon suffering as St. Paul did:

I consider the sufferings of the present to be as nothing compared with the glory to be revealed in us (Rom. 8:18).*

And St. James said:

Happy the man who stands firm when trials come. He has proved himself, and will win the prize of life, the crown that the Lord has promised to those who love him (Jas. 1:12).** (See also: 1 Pt. 4:16; Rom. 12:14, 21.)

HOW DO WE LIVE OUR FAITH?

We live our faith by studying our religion, by making frequent acts of faith, and by showing faith in good actions.

I live in faith: faith in the Son of God who loved me and who sacrificed himself for my sake (Gal. 2:20).**

We live our faith by avoiding whatever endangers it, such as bad companions, the reading of bad literature, pride of mind and heart. These can lead to denial of some or all the truths of faith, or indifference in the practice of our faith.

HOW DO WE SHOW OUR FAITH IN ACTION?

We show our faith in action by bringing the Gospel spirit into every aspect of our life, especially to our relations with our fellow man. We thus witness to Christ and contribute to extending the kingdom of God and building a more human world.

Should anyone ask you the reason for this hope of yours, be ever ready to reply (1 Pt. 3:15).*

WHAT DOES ST. JAMES SAY ABOUT CHRISTIANS WHO DO NOT REFLECT THE GOSPEL SPIRIT IN THEIR LIVES?

Nobody must imagine that he is religious while he still goes on deceiving himself and not keeping control over his tongue; anyone who does this has the wrong idea of religion (Jas. 1:26).**

WHAT ARE THE WALKS OF LIFE IN WHICH CHRISTIANS MAY SERVE GOD AND THEIR NEIGHBOR?

The walks of life in which Christians may grow close to God and love their neighbor are: priesthood and/or religious life, married life, the single state.

ARE THERE ANY LIFE-LONG COMMITMENTS BESIDES THE MARRIED STATE AND PRIESTHOOD?

Besides marriage and priesthood, other life-long commitments are the calls to the religious life as a priest, brother or sister and the vocation to a secular institute.

WHAT IS A "VOCATION"?

A vocation is God's calling of a person to a particular way of life, especially the priesthood or religious life.

"As the Father has sent me,
so I send you" (Jn. 20:21).* (See also: Jn. 15:16.)

WHAT IS RELIGIOUS LIFE?

Religious life is a special way of following Jesus. Religious are persons who make the vows of chastity, obedience and poverty in a religious community.

WHAT IS A VOW?

A vow is a free and deliberate promise made to God by which a person binds himself under pain of sin to do something which is possible, morally good, and better than its voluntary omission.

WHAT VOWS DO RELIGIOUS MAKE?

Religious make three vows: chastity (not to marry), poverty (to give up material goods), obedience (to obey their superiors, who hold God's place). These vows are called evangelical counsels.

WHAT IS THE PURPOSE OF THE RELIGIOUS VOWS?

Religious vows are meant to free the mind and heart of the religious so that he or she can love God entirely and serve His people full time.

HOW CAN WE HELP THE MISSIONS?

We can help the missions by prayer, contributions and sacrifices.

IS EVERY PRIEST CALLED A RELIGIOUS?

Not every priest is called a religious. Only those priests who belong to a religious congregation are called religious. Priests who do not belong to a religious congregation are called diocesan priests or parish priests because they are dedicated to ministering to the People of God in parishes.

IS EVERY BROTHER AND SISTER CALLED A RELIGIOUS?

Every brother and sister is called a religious because each belongs to a religious congregation.

DO RELIGIOUS RECEIVE A SPECIAL SACRAMENT?

Religious priests receive the sacrament of Holy Orders, but religious life itself does not have a "special" sacrament. Religious make public profession of three vows of poverty, chastity and obedience in imitation of Jesus. Religious also promise to serve the Church by their dedication to the particular apostolic labors to which their religious congregation is dedicated.

WHAT DOES RELIGIOUS CHASTITY MEAN?

Religious chastity is the name of the vow made by religious, who freely dedicate their whole lives to God forgoing marriage and family life. St. Paul says:

An unmarried man can devote himself to the Lord's affairs, all he need worry about is pleasing the Lord (1 Cor. 7:32).**

WHAT DOES RELIGIOUS POVERTY MEAN?

Religious poverty is the name of a promise or vow made by religious in which they choose to renounce the ownership of the goods of this earth, and share things in common so that they will find their "treasure" in heaven (cf. Mt. 19:16-22).

WHAT DOES RELIGIOUS OBEDIENCE MEAN?

Religious obedience is the special vow by which religious pledge to obey the Rule of their religious congregation and their superior who they know represents God for them.

WHAT IS "COMMUNITY LIFE"?

"Community life," an essential factor in religious life, is the religious community's serene living together, sharing the same life of prayer, labor, the same food, accommodations, and schedule, united in a common ideal.

WHAT IS THE ORIGIN OF RELIGIOUS LIFE?

The origin of religious life is rooted in Sacred Scripture and most especially, in the words and examples of Jesus, the Divine Master. To the rich young man Jesus said:

"If you seek perfection, go, sell your possessions, and give to the poor. You will then have treasure in heaven. Afterward, come back and follow me" (Mt. 19:21).* (See also: Mt. 5:48, Lk. 18:28-30.)

WHAT IS THE PURPOSE OF RELIGIOUS LIFE?

The purpose of religious life is to give glory to God and to pursue personal sanctification by imitating the life of Jesus, the Divine Master. Jesus said:

"In a word, you must be made perfect as your heavenly Father is perfect" (Mt. 5:48).* (See also: 1 Thes. 4:3; Mt. 19:21.)

WHAT KIND OF REWARD DOES JESUS PROMISE TO THE FAITHFUL RELIGIOUS PRIESTS, BROTHERS AND SISTERS?

Jesus spoke of the reward thus:

"...There is no one who has left home or wife or brothers, parents or children, for the sake of the kingdom of God who will not receive a plentiful return in this age and life everlasting in the age to come" (Lk. 18:29-30).*

Index

Daughters of St. Paul

IN MASSACHUSETTS
  50 St. Paul's Ave. Jamaica Plain, Boston, MA 02130;
    617-522-8911; 617-522-0875;
  172 Tremont Street, Boston, MA 02111; **617-426-5464;**
    617-426-4230
IN NEW YORK
  78 Fort Place, Staten Island, NY 10301; **212-447-5071**
  59 East 43rd Street, New York, NY 10017; **212-986-7580**
  7 State Street, New York, NY 10004; **212-447-5086**
  625 East 187th Street, Bronx, NY 10458; **212-584-0440**
  525 Main Street, Buffalo, NY 14203; **716-847-6044**
IN NEW JERSEY
  Hudson Mall — Route 440 and Communipaw Ave.,
    Jersey City, NJ 07304; **201-433-7740**
IN CONNECTICUT
  202 Fairfield Ave., Bridgeport, CT 06604; **203-335-9913**
IN OHIO
  2105 Ontario St. (at Prospect Ave.), Cleveland, OH 44115; **216-621-9427**
  25 E. Eighth Street, Cincinnati, OH 45202; **513-721-4838**
IN PENNSYLVANIA
  1719 Chestnut Street, Philadelphia, PA 19103; **215-568-2638**
IN FLORIDA
  2700 Biscayne Blvd., Miami, FL 33137; **305-573-1618**
IN LOUISIANA
  4403 Veterans Memorial Blvd., Metairie, LA 70002; **504-887-7631;**
    504-887-0113
  1800 South Acadian Thruway, P.O. Box 2028, Baton Rouge, LA 70821
    504-343-4057; 504-343-3814
IN MISSOURI
  1001 Pine Street (at North 10th), St. Louis, MO 63101; **314-621-0346;**
    314-231-5522
IN ILLINOIS
  172 North Michigan Ave., Chicago, IL 60601; **312-346-4228**
IN TEXAS
  114 Main Plaza, San Antonio, TX 78205; **512-224-8101**
IN CALIFORNIA
  1570 Fifth Avenue, San Diego, CA 92101; **714-232-1442**
  46 Geary Street, San Francisco, CA 94108; **415-781-5180**
IN HAWAII
  1143 Bishop Street, Honolulu, HI 96813; **808-521-2731**
IN ALASKA
  750 West 5th Avenue, Anchorage AK 99501; **907-272-8183**
IN CANADA
  3022 Dufferin Street, Toronto 395, Ontario, Canada
IN ENGLAND
  57, Kensington Church Street, London W. 8, England
IN AUSTRALIA
  58 Abbotsford Rd., Homebush, N.S.W., Sydney 2140, Australia